Stadium Stories:

Michigan Wolverines

Colorful Tales of the Maize and Blue

Jim Cnockaert

The Globe Pequot Press

GUILFORD, CONNECTICUT

Text design: Casey Shain
Cover photos courtesy of the *Ann Arbor News* and Bentley Historical Library

Library of Congress Cataloging-in-Publication Data
Cnockaert, Jim.
    Stadium stories : Michigan Wolverines / Jim Cnockaert.
        p. cm.
    ISBN 0-7627-2784-5
        1. Michigan Wolverines (Football team)—History.
2. University of Michigan—Football—History. I. Title.

GV958.U52863C56 2003
796.332'63'0977435—dc21   2003054703

Manufactured in the United States of America
First Edition/First Printing

To the women in my life: my mother, Albina, the first to suggest I take up writing as a career; my wife, Christine, who inspires, encourages, and edits me; and, my daughters, Anne, Susan, and Emily, whose energy and enthusiasm help keep me young.

Contents

Acknowledgments

This book would not have been possible without the assistance and support of a number of people, and I want to thank them.

David Ablauf, of the University of Michigan sports information department, and Brian Reynolds, of the *Ann Arbor News* photo department, helped me to locate most of the photographs and download them onto CDs.

My wife and computer guru, Christine Uthoff, got me past all technical hurdles.

Ann Arbor News publisher Dave Sharp, editor Ed Petykiewicz and sports editor Jim Knight provided the encouragement I needed to complete this project. Heather Feldkamp, the *News'* business development manager, was a dynamo in helping to promote the book.

Mike Urban, Mary Norris, and Josh Rosenberg of The Globe Pequot Press provided a lot of advice. They, too, offered encouragement.

Dr. Bill Graves provided a wealth of Michigan football information.

Finally, I would like to thank the many members of the Michigan teams of 1947, 1950, 1969, and 1980 who so generously granted interviews and shared their stories. Without them, this book and some of the Michigan football history it chronicles could not have been written.

Michigan and Its Traditions

"You Can't Have One without the Other"

Tradition. There simply is no way to describe more than a century of University of Michigan football without coming back to this word.

It is cavernous Michigan Stadium, the largest college-owned facility of its kind in the nation. It is the distinctive winged helmets, worn by Michigan teams since 1938. It is the maize-and-blue colors, adopted by students in 1867. It is the school fight song, "The Victors," which has been a staple of football Saturdays in Ann Arbor since Louis Elbel wrote it in 1898 and John Philip Sousa first performed it in 1899. It is the smart-stepping Michigan Marching Band, which still charges out of the stadium tunnel and forms a huge block "M" to start every pregame show.

Then, there are the wins and the championships. No Division I team in college football history has won more games than Michigan. No program has won more Big Ten championships. No Big Ten team has been to the Rose Bowl more often.

Tradition. It is the building block of athletic excellence. It, as much or more than anything else, explains why the fight song refers to Michigan as "the leaders and best," and fans and alumni accept that definition without question. It also helps to explain why the Wolverines haven't played to a home crowd of less than 100,000 fans since 1975.

Tradition. It's what prompted former coach and athletic director Fielding H. Yost to once assert that Michigan's proper place in college football was above all others. When other coaches would ask Yost to reveal his morale-making secrets, he replied: "You don't put morale on like a coat. You build it day by day."

Tradition. It's what Michigan football coaches have sold to recruits and preached to their players for decades. When push comes to shove, they'd say, the Wolverines find a way to win because that's what Michigan teams have always done.

Asked once what he believed set Michigan football apart, Coach Lloyd Carr talked first and foremost about tradition. "[Fritz] Crisler said it can't be bottled and it isn't something bought at the corner store, but it's there to sustain you in times of need," Carr said. "One thing I really believe in is the spirit of men like that . . . their love for the university, their love for the guys who played the game, and their will to win. Those are the things that set them apart. I feel a real sense of obligation because I believe in that tradition."

This book explores aspects of Michigan's tradition, particularly some of the coaches, the players, and the teams that helped to create and shape a legacy that is second to none in college football. It is only a small sampling. A complete history of the football program would fill volumes.

First, however, it is worth examining some of the things that make Michigan football special.

The Winged Helmet

Fritz Crisler, the head coach from 1938–47, was an innovator. He brought about two-platoon football, and he invented many

Michigan's winged helmets
(Ann Arbor News)

of the formations and wrote many of the rules that are still used today. But his greatest contribution to the Michigan football tradition arguably was the introduction of the winged helmet, a design regarded as the most recognized and distinctive in college football.

Before Crisler arrived in 1938 from Princeton, Michigan used black helmets and, like most teams of the day, wore dark, solid uniforms. Crisler wanted to "dress them up" and give them distinction, so he had the helmets painted in their distinctive maize-and-blue winged pattern, with the maize highlighting the stitching of the leather helmets.

The change was much more than cosmetic. Crisler believed the design would help passers spot their receivers downfield. Crisler later recalled: "There was a tendency to use different-colored helmets just for receivers in those days, but I always thought that would be as helpful for the defense as for the offense."

The change paid immediate dividends. In Crisler's first season Michigan nearly doubled its passing yards, increased its completion percentage, and cut its interceptions nearly in half from the previous season.

Why Wolverines?

Michigan students and alumni have referred to themselves as Wolverines since the earliest recorded history of the university, but no one knows for certain why the nickname was chosen for the school's athletic teams.

The logical explanation would be that the nickname was chosen because the animal was indigenous to the state of Michigan, but it is not. Instead, there are several theories as to why the nickname was chosen.

Former coach and athletic director Fielding H. Yost believed the nickname might have had something to do with the trading of wolverine pelts at Sault Sainte Marie among Indians, trappers, and merchants. Traders might have referred to the pelts as "Michigan wolverines." Another theory, presented in the *Michigan Quarterly Review* in 1952, suggested that the early French settlers had gluttonous, or "wolverine-like," appetites. The third theory surrounds the Michigan–Ohio border dispute of 1803, during which Michiganders were called "wolverines," though it is unclear whether the name was a flattering one or considered an insult.

In 1923 Yost became captivated by the Wisconsin team's practice of carrying about a live badger as a mascot, and he resolved to get a live wolverine for Michigan. His failure to find one only stimulated his search. When a questionnaire sent to sixty-eight trappers produced nothing, he contacted every Michigan letterman in the state. When that produced no results, he researched books, contacted animal experts, and even consulted politicians. He visited one state senator who reportedly owned a stuff wolverine, but it turned out that the beast was a coyote. Desperate, Yost extended his search into Canada, and he eventually was able to obtain a twenty-six-pound stuffed wolverine from a man in Hudson's Bay, Ontario. Still, Yost was tormented by his desire to have a live wolverine.

In 1927 he obtained ten live wolverines from Alaska and placed them at the Detroit Zoo. On football days, two of the animals would be brought in cages to Michigan Stadium. However, the animals grew so vicious that Yost had to give up on them, and he shipped all but one of them out to zoos. "It was obvious that the Michigan mascots had designs on the Michigan men toting them, and those designs were by no means friendly," Yost later recalled. The one wolverine Yost kept, nicknamed "Biff," was put on display at the University of Michigan Zoo.

In 1937 the Chevrolet Motor Company donated a live wolverine and a cage to keep it in to the university. It is unclear how long this animal lived, but the practice of bringing a live mascot to the stadium ended more than a half-century ago.

The Michigan Marching Band

Fielding H. Yost, who became football coach in 1901, first instilled the belief that the Wolverines' proper place in college football should be above all others. He could have said the same thing about the Michigan Marching Band. Like the football team, the marching band's list of firsts is a long one.

- The band created the first "Script Ohio" to honor the relationship between Michigan and Ohio State, and it performed the formation during the 1932 game in Ohio Stadium. The formation would later be made famous by Ohio State's marching band.
- The Michigan Marching Band was the first to perform in the Rose Bowl, on January 1, 1948. It has performed in Pasadena during every Michigan visit since.
- The band was the first Big Ten marching band to appear in a Super Bowl (1973). It also appeared during the 1982 Super Bowl at the Pontiac Silverdome.
- The band was nicknamed "The Transcontinental Marching Band" after it appeared in both Yankee Stadium (for a game against Army) and the Rose Bowl during the 1950 season. No marching band had ever done that before.
- The band received the inaugural Louis Sudler National Intercollegiate Marching Band Trophy in 1983. The trophy is now awarded annually to a college marching band of particular excellence. The trophy was the brainchild of Louis Sudler, a Chicago realtor and vice-chair of the John

Philip Sousa Foundation. Finalists for the award were selected by more than 700 marching band directors, as well as sportswriters and television commentators, and the winner was selected by a panel of twenty marching band directors from around the country.

The marching band began as an entirely student-run organization in the fall of 1896. Though previous attempts to start a band had failed because of a lack of support, Ann Arbor student Harry dePont invited all musicians on campus to attend an organizational meeting. Nearly thirty musicians did.

Convinced that a suitable home for the band would be the key to maintaining interest among musicians, dePont approached school president James Burrill Angell, a close family friend, to ask that the university provide a rehearsal site. Angell said he was glad to assist, but he wanted a demonstration that the band was a "sincere venture." The band provided it, performing at the Law School's annual observance of Washington's Birthday in 1897. Angell granted permission for the band to rehearse in University Hall, where the group became a distraction to other students because the walls were not soundproof. The band eventually settled into the fencing room at Waterman Gymnasium. The band would play that spring at track meets and baseball games—fast becoming one of the most popular groups on campus—and it entertained at the Evening Promenade, the most important social event during commencement week.

The band began the 1897–98 school year with musicians still providing their own instruments and music racks, and organizers announced that uniforms were "still a thing of the future." The band helped rouse enthusiasm at the first mass campus meeting of the new football season by performing several lively two-step numbers. Wearing blue serge coats, white duck pants, and "M" caps that were purchased the previous spring, the band accompanied the football team to Detroit that November for a game against Minnesota.

By the following fall the band had become an indispensable presence at football games, and that included traveling to road games. After a come-from-behind win against the University of Chicago in the season finale, the band led a postgame celebration through the streets of Chicago. It was during this revelry that a Michigan student, Louis Elbel, was inspired to compose the school's now famous fight song, "The Victors."

The university provided no financial support for the band for nearly two decades, so the band's existence depended on the generosity of the community and the savvy of its conductors. In the summer of 1915, the university announced it had hired Wilfred Wilson to serve as band conductor and would pay his salary. Wilson had spent his career with bands in the U.S. Army and at several military academies, and he instilled discipline and high musical standards in the Michigan band. By the time he left Ann Arbor in 1926, the band had grown from forty to nearly one hundred members.

The band's pre-Wilson reputation was enhanced in 1914 by the introduction of a drum major. The first was George Olsen, a sixteen-year-old saxophone player from Portland, Oregon, whose military prep school background and drum-and-bugle-corps experience made him the ideal candidate for the position. Olsen's first appearance at the head of the band prompted laughter from spectators, but he soon became popular. During a game against Syracuse at Ferry Field that season, Olsen led the band onto the field. Fans were fascinated by the way Olsen twirled his baton, and they cheered him loudly. He became so excited that he threw the baton over the crossbar of the goalpost, and he luckily caught it on the other side.

The crowd assumed it was a planned stunt, and another tradition was born.

The arrival of William Revelli in 1935 sparked new life for the band. Revelli recruited musicians like a football coach did players. When World War II began, most university bands throughout the country ceased operations. The Michigan band did not. Half-time themes were patriotic and supportive of the home-front victory programs. After the war the band introduced faster tempos and a new high-step marching style that caught the attention of the nation when the band performed at the 1948 Rose Bowl. The band's first pregame entry through the Michigan Stadium tunnel at a rapid cadence was also performed in 1948.

In 1952 former Michigan bandsman George Cavender returned to his alma mater to assist Revelli. The two soon enlisted another former band member, Jerry Bilik, whose genius for arranging helped produced several of the band's traditional and favorite numbers: "M Fanfare," "Temptation," and "Hawaiian War Chant." During this period the band became the most imitated and admired marching band in the nation.

Change continued in the 1970s. When Revelli retired in 1971, the Michigan bands consisted of six bands, with an enrollment of nearly 500 students. That year, Carl Grapentine, an oboist in the School of Music, began his career as "The Voice of the Michigan Marching Band." In 1972 women were finally admitted to the marching band. By the beginning of the new millennium, a woman would become drum major.

"The Victors"

Michigan's come-from-behind 12–11 win against Amos Alonzo Stagg's powerful University of Chicago team in 1898 not only gave the Wolverines their first-ever Big Nine

Conference championship, it would inspire a student to compose what John Philip Sousa would later call the finest college fight song ever written.

One of the 1,400 fans attending the game at Chicago's Marshall Field that day was Louis Elbel. During a celebration by Michigan fans in the streets of Chicago, Elbel was struck by the fact that his university did not have the right celebration song. Walking back to a relative's house that night, the melody popped into his head. He wrote his thoughts down on paper and then tried them out on the piano the following night. He got the idea to make the song into a march—and did so—on the train trip back to Ann Arbor.

Sheet music for "The Victors"
(Bentley Historical Library)

He later recalled: "There was never a more enthusiastic Michigan student than I, but that team and that Chicago game pushed me way up in the clouds, and all I had to do was fill in the notes, and there was 'The Victors'."

Elbel would have been content just to write the song, but his brother, who was in the music business, encouraged him to have it printed. After printed copies were received in early April 1899, Elbel asked Sousa if he would consider having his band play the march at a scheduled concert at Michigan's University Hall on April 8. Sousa agreed to perform the debut. Two nights later "The Victors" was performed by an orchestra at the UM Minstrels concert. It was during this performance that the words were sung for the first time.

The Little Brown Jug

The oldest and most famous trophy in Division I college football is neither little, nor brown.

The Jug stands about 2 feet tall, weighs about fifteen pounds, and when it was actually used as a jug, held five gallons of water. The day in 1903 when a Michigan team manager purchased it from a Minneapolis variety store for 30 cents, it was putty colored. It has long since been painted over with the colors of the two schools that play for it: maize and blue for Michigan; maroon and gold for Minnesota.

Whether the name fits has never been an issue for players or coaches who have competed for the Jug. It is a tangible piece of college football history, one that represents the proud traditions of both schools. It is, as former Minnesota athletic director L. J. Cooke once said, "the embodiment of the spirit of anyone who ever played for it."

Yost's Michigan team was riding a twenty-eight-game winning streak, and Minnesota was 10–0 when the teams played in 1903 in Minneapolis before more than 20,000 boisterous spectators. Having doubts that Minnesota would provide pure water for his players, Yost dispatched a team manager, Tommy Roberts, to purchase something—the Jug—that could be filled with water.

The game was one of the most physical of its day, but Michigan took a 6–0 lead with twelve minutes remaining in the game on a short touchdown run by Joe Maddock. But the Gophers tied the game with two minutes remaining on a touchdown run by reserve fullback Egil Boeckmann. Spectators rushed the field, and the game was called with time still remaining. In its haste to leave, the Michigan team left the Jug behind.

Minnesota equipment manager Oscar Munson discovered the Jug the morning after the game and brought it to

Marcus Ray (29), Sam Sword, and Charles Woodson (2) celebrate with the Little Brown Jug after a 24–3 win against Minnesota in 1997. (Ann Arbor News)

Cooke, the athletic director. To commemorate the tie, Cooke had the Jug painted with the score and the inscription "Michigan Jug—Captured by Oscar, October 31, 1903" and put it on display.

For reasons that are unclear, Yost sent a letter to Cooke asking that the Jug be returned. Cooke wrote back: "If you want it, you'll have to come up and win it." Because of the brutality of the 1903 game, the teams did not play again until 1909, when the Wolverines won it back with a 15–6 win.

Unlike the Paul Bunyan Trophy, which is exchanged between Michigan and Michigan State in the locker room after a game, the Jug is paraded on the field. The Wolverines

Where It All Started

Michigan played its first football game May 30, 1879, against Racine College of Wisconsin. The game was played exactly a decade after the first college football game ever, between Princeton and Rutgers.

Michigan and Racine officials agreed on a neutral site, White Stocking Park in Chicago. A crowd of about 500 spectators watched Michigan post its first victory. Irving K. Pond, who later would design the Michigan Union and the Michigan League buildings, scored the first touchdown, but Dave DeTarr missed the point-after try for a goal—at least officially.

Michigan's student newspaper, the *Chronicle,* took exception to a referee's decision on the DeTarr kick: "A kick was made by Captain DeTarr for the goal, which, according to the referee's decision, missed; but our umpire and the whole team and spectators declared the goal was safely made. . . . We do not wish to dispute with the referee, yet, we must suggest, he is as liable to be mistaken as anyone else."

DeTarr did get a second chance. With two minutes remaining, he successfully place-kicked a goal that proved to be the difference. Michigan won the game, 1–0.

Michigan's Milestone Wins

Win	Date	Opponent	Score
1	May 30, 1879	Racine	1–0
50	November 29, 1894	Chicago	12–0
100	October 5, 1901	Case	57–0
200	October 9, 1915	Mt. Union	35–0
300	October 1, 1932	Michigan State	26–0
400	October 23, 1948	Minnesota	27–14
500	November 11, 1967	Illinois	21–14
600	October 21, 1978	Wisconsin	42–0
700	November 4, 1989	Purdue	42–27
750	September 9, 1995	Memphis	24–7
800	September 30, 2000	Wisconsin	13–10

have done most of the parading lately: They lost the Jug just twice during the last three decades of the twentieth century. The lopsidedness of the series prompted Minnesota coach Glen Mason to remark before the 2002 game (another Michigan win): "I've never seen the darn thing, so it's hard to comment on it. I'd like to get it back just to see it and touch it."

When the Jug is in Michigan's hands, it is kept under tight security in Schembechler Hall. Michigan officials are sensitive about the Jug's safety because it was stolen from the athletic department in 1930 and went missing for four years. The Jug eventually was recovered by an Ann Arbor gas station attendant, who found it behind a clump of bushes. One official suspects a Michigan student took the Jug and kept it until graduating from the university.

The Jug has been stored for many decades in a metal case that, like the Jug, is painted in the colors of the two schools. The padded interior of the case is lined with red velvet. It is unclear which school had the case constructed.

Each Sunday before a Minnesota game, Michigan players are briefed on the Jug's history. If the Jug is in the Wolverines' possession, players are allowed to touch it. Then, it is put away until game day, when it is kept near the team bench.

"Every time I take the Jug out, I think: 'Man, the stories it could tell if it could just talk,' " Michigan director of equipment operations Jon Falk said in a 2002 interview with the *Ann Arbor News*. "Just think of the people who have handled it, all the team captains and coaches and players."

The Men Who Molded Michigan

Yost, Crisler, and Schembechler

The three coaches who did the most to create and define the Michigan football tradition—Fielding H. Yost, Fritz Crisler, and Bo Schembechler—originally were not Michigan men at all.

Yost, a University of West Virginia graduate who also attended Ohio Northern and Lafayette, came to Ann Arbor via Stanford, Nebraska, Kansas, and Ohio Wesleyan. Crisler, a University of Chicago alumnus, previously had coached at Princeton and Minnesota. Schembechler, who played under Woody Hayes at Miami of Ohio and later coached for him as an assistant at Ohio State, came to Michigan after six seasons at his alma mater.

No matter what their backgrounds, however, they will forever be linked to the Wolverines.

Yost was the architect. His "Point-a-Minute" teams, which played fifty-six games without a loss from 1901–05, began the winningest tradition in college football. During his long tenure as athletic director, Yost built athletic facilities, including Michigan Stadium, that were second to none in the nation.

Crisler was an innovator. He designed Michigan's famed winged helmets—the most recognized in college football—and implemented the "two-platoon system" that changed the college and professional games forever. His undefeated 1947 team, nicknamed the "Mad Magicians," is regarded by some as the finest team the school has ever produced.

Schembechler restored Michigan to greatness. His first team, in 1969, stunned top-ranked and defending national champion Ohio State in what is considered one of the greatest upsets in college football history. His teams would win or tie for thirteen Big Ten championships in twenty-one seasons. In the two decades prior to his arrival, Michigan won just two conference titles.

In the process the three men left a legacy of excellence and success by which all Michigan teams are measured.

Fielding H. Yost

A friend once asked Ring Lardner if he'd ever talked with Fielding Yost. Lardner replied: "No, my father taught me never to interrupt." Columnist Grantland Rice once bet Herbert Bayard Swope, the editor of the old *New York World*, that Yost could outtalk him. Swope took the bet and lost, later admitting, "Every time I try to sneak in a word, he just drowns me out."

One reason Yost talked so much was that he knew so much—about football, war, history, business, you name it. Friends said he could have been a millionaire had he concentrated on business, a five-star general if he had chosen the military as a career, or an actor to rival the greatest of all time had he picked the stage.

Fortunately for Michigan, he chose football. In twenty-five seasons as Michigan's head coach, his teams were 165–29–10. His first five teams, which compiled a combined 55–1–1 record and scored 2,821 points to opponents' 42, might just be the best assembled by one coach at one school.

Yost's middle name was Harris, but the "H" quickly came to stand for his nickname "Hurry Up." Michigan football lore has it that as soon as he arrived by train in Ann Arbor, Yost grabbed his bags and dashed up the hill to campus, the sooner to get to work. But former Michigan player Paul Jones, a member of the 1901 team, recalled decades later that Yost got his nickname because of the sense of urgency he instilled

Fielding H. Yost (Ann Arbor News)

in his players. "[Quarterback] Boss Weeks would call signals for the next play while he was still under the pile of the previous scrimmage," Jones said. "If you did not get into the play fast enough, Yost would shout at you from the sidelines, 'Are you just a spectator? Hurry up, hurry up!' That is how his name originated."

Rival coaches had other ideas about the nickname. Illinois's Bob Zuppke once said: "Don't give me any of the Fielding 'Harris' Yost stuff. His name is Fielding 'Hitting' Yost. His teams knock you down and run away from you, but when you try the same thing on them, they knock you down again."

The nickname had yet another meaning. Yost did not believe in "rebuilding" a program. Wherever he coached, he expected to win immediately, and he did. In 1900, the year before Michigan hired Yost, the Wolverines were 7–2–1, but they lost to rival Chicago and finished fifth in the Western Conference (now called the Big Ten). In 1901 the Wolverines won all eleven games, outscored opponents 550–0, and hammered Stanford 49–0 in the first Rose Bowl game.

Military history fascinated Yost. Once, curious whether the defeat of the Seventh Cavalry at the Battle of the Little Big Horn had been General George Armstrong Custer's fault, he went to the site of Custer's Last Stand to interview surviving Indians. He was an expert on the Civil War, and he admired Stonewall Jackson and Robert E. Lee.

Having the Last Word

Fielding Yost's "punt, pass, and pray" offense was hailed as just the trick when Michigan was winning consistently. But, whenever the Wolverines would hit a losing streak, critics carped at the dullness of the "Triple P" attack.

Never one to take criticism easily, Yost bit back: "We play percentage. We let the other fellow rush the ball and waste his energy in his own territory. Football games aren't won—they're lost. And Meeshegan's record is due to a policy of letting the enemy take the risk of fumbling inside his 40. Then we cash in on his mistakes. Let 'em holler about a punt, a pass, and a prayer. We generally have the last laugh."

What his knowledge and experiences taught him was, that to be successful in any endeavor, you had to be a stickler for details. That was particularly true in football. He often counseled his players: "Many have the will to win, but few have the will to prepare." Nothing escaped his attention, and he expected his players to be just as diligent. Yost once told quarterback Benny Friedman: "They might outpower us, Benny, but they can't outsmart us."

Yost first instilled the belief—embraced by alums and despised by opponents—that Michigan's proper place in college football should be above all others. As one of his squads would leave the dressing room to take the field immediately before a game, Yost would say of an opponent: "Who are they to beat a Michigan team? They are only human."

That attitude—some called it arrogance—was only part of the reason for Yost's success. He pioneered changes in philosophy and tactics that are still in use. For instance, he introduced the no-huddle offense before the 1902 Rose Bowl game against Stanford. In his 1905 book *Football for Player and Spectator*, Yost wrote: "Football is being made more and more a game of physical and mental skill, rather than a contest of mere force." He believed that speed, intelligence, and the element of surprise were more important than size. He often remarked: "It takes less effort to fool 'em than it does to knock 'em down."

Fans often accused Yost of boring them with his play calling, which was referred to as "punt, pass, and pray." He liked to punt a down earlier than usual, so his teams often sacrificed first downs for the prospect of better field position. Yost would answer such complaints: "Don'tcha know, it isn't the first downs that count. It's the touchdowns." Yost liked to play the percentages, and he was often content to let an opponent take the risks and allow his team to capitalize on mistakes. "Football games aren't won—they're lost," he said.

As noteworthy as his football accomplishments are, Yost left an even greater legacy to his university in terms of the facilities he built and the manner in which he ran the athletic department. Yost conceived and engineered Michigan's athletic campus. Among the projects constructed under Yost's direction were Michigan Stadium, the university's eighteen-hole golf course, the nation's first intramural sports building, and the nation's first multipurpose field house (now Yost Ice Arena).

"I'm interested in fitness for all," Yost told Michigan manager of athletics Charles Baird the day he arrived in Ann Arbor. "Athletics for all—that's Meeshegan's motto now that Yost is here."

Fritz Crisler

His players used to call him "The Lord." Some of that surely was out of awe or fear, but there was never a doubt it also was out of respect. When Fritz Crisler spoke, no one said a word. He never swore. He didn't have to. His look said it all. And one of his stares was enough to get a player's attention.

"I think I probably tried to remember and emulate those things he believed in," said Chalmers "Bump" Elliott, a member of Crisler's 1947 team who would later become Michigan's head coach. "He was a fairly serious person, but he had a great sense of humor. We all had a great respect for him, because we recognized his great knowledge of the game."

Though he coached at Michigan for just ten seasons, Crisler was such an innovator and student of football that he would give the Wolverines a new identity and change the college game forever.

When he arrived from Princeton in 1938, Crisler scrapped Michigan's old black helmets in favor of a distinctive winged design still worn by the team today. Crisler said he'd changed the look because he wanted to dress the helmet up a little bit, but there also was a practical application. Crisler knew the unique helmet would help his passers spot their receivers downfield more easily.

Michigan coach Fritz Crisler
(Ann Arbor News)

Crisler was the first coach to use platoon football: one unit for offense and one for defense. For decades teams had played "iron man football," which meant eleven players on each team usually played the entire game. The rules were changed in 1941 to allow a player to enter the game at any time, but no one recognized the potential of the rule until Crisler took advantage of it in 1945 "out of sheer necessity." Recognizing that his team of youngsters would be overmatched physically in a game at Yankee Stadium against a powerhouse Army team led by Doc Blanchard and Glenn Davis, Crisler picked his best defensive players for one unit and his best offensive players for the other. The idea, he said, was to keep all of them fresh. Though he only wound up platooning his lines and linebackers in that game, the system worked. The game was tied 7–7 in the third quarter, before Army finally wore down the

Wolverines for a 28–7 win. "It could have been much worse," Crisler said.

The move stunned the college football world, and it wasn't long before coaches realized Crisler had begun a revolution. For weeks after the game, Crisler's telephone rang constantly. Coaches wanted to know how the system worked. Some other coaches tried it that same season. A year later Army had gone to a two-platoon system.

His given name was Herbert Orin Crisler. A native of Earlville, Illinois, he never participated in athletics before college because he was too skinny. He weighed one hundred pounds when he graduated from high school. He earned a scholarship to attend the University of Chicago, where he planned to study medicine, but he gained enough weight to go out for sports. He would earn nine letters—one of only two Chicago athletes to do so—playing football, baseball, and basketball.

The nickname "Fritz" was given to him during his sopho-more football season by Chicago's legendary coach, Amos Alonzo Stagg. Frustrated by Crisler's consistent bungling of a new play, Stagg identified Crisler with a celebrated violinist who had a similar last name, Kreisler. Stagg told Crisler: "[Kreisler] has certain attributes and he knows how to use them. He has genius, skill, coordination. From now on, Crisler, I'm going to call you Fritz, too, just to remind myself that you are absolutely his opposite." Crisler would prove Stagg wrong, but the nickname stuck.

Crisler learned much from Stagg, both as a player and during eight seasons as an assistant coach. He admired the way Stagg motivated players, including himself, and he would later use those same tactics at Minnesota, Princeton, and Michigan. What Crisler didn't like was the way Stagg ran practices, which tended to run long and lacked discipline and order. Crisler would change that when he became head coach.

His practices at Michigan were planned to the minute detail. Players recall that he carried a notepad of 3-by-5-inch cards in his hip pocket on which he had written down a timed-out schedule of that day's practice. Items were written either in red or blue ink, with anything in red being the most important. He would make notes on the pad during practice, and then file the cards away afterward for future reference.

Bobby Mann, a member of the 1947 team, recalled that the Wolverines would be forced to repeatedly practice a play until Crisler was satisfied with their technique. Sometimes, it was a back who had to repeat a running play until he had perfected the technique of running a full half-yard closer to a double-team block. At other times it was a pass receiver who had to repeat a pass play until he learned to cut up the field just at 12½ yards—not at 12 yards, nor at 13 yards.

Mann's teammate, Bob Chappuis, had similar recollections: "There were three words I remember coming out of his mouth frequently: 'Run it again.' He had this raised platform he stood on. We'd run a play, and if he wasn't satisfied, he'd say, 'Run it again. Run it again.' We ran it again until we were tired of it."

But the preparation paid off. Elliott recalled that Crisler's planning for a game was completely thorough. Nothing was left to chance. The Wolverines all believed that when they completed the week's practices for an opponent, their game plan was perfect. To a man, Crisler's former players say they always believed they were better prepared than their opponents. Elliott recalled: "On Saturday morning Fritz would talk to the team, and his final thoughts usually included these words: 'Men, ours is a simple plan; theirs is a plan of

What Have You Done for Us Lately?

After leading his 1947 team to a decisive Rose Bowl victory over Southern Cal in what would prove to be his final game as head coach, Fritz Crisler was understandably jubilant. A disgruntled Michigan fan had a different perspective on the game, however.

During an *Ann Arbor News* interview in 1979, Crisler recalled: "One of the most amusing things about that game was what happened afterward as I was walking to the dressing room. This young fella, he was from Michigan, came up and said, 'We have to do something about the coaching.' I said, 'What's wrong? We won the game, didn't we?' He said, 'Well, in 1902 we played Stanford and won 49–0. Look what happened today. We play USC, and we win 49–0. We haven't improved a damn bit in 46 years.' "

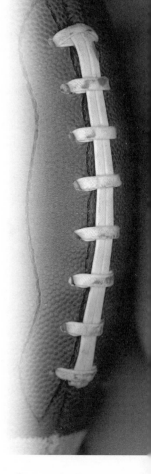

desperation. . . . Our preparation is complete, and when you follow our plan you will win.' This kind of complete belief gave our teams absolute confidence."

Crisler's pregame pep talks weren't all business. As Yost before him, Crisler had a knack for saying whatever his team needed to hear at that moment to inspire it. Pete Elliott recalled that players would wait for and listen to Crisler's every word, even his pauses, which were dramatic and meaningful. In a 1996 letter about Crisler, Albert Wistert recalled: "Before the Michigan State game one year, he said, 'Nobody ever heard of Michigan State before they beat us. You made them. Now, I want you to go out there and break them!' " Against Minnesota one year, he said, 'This game will take all you've got—60 minutes of unrelenting, everlasting pressure, 60 minutes of sacrifice, and a lifetime to remember!' "

Crisler coached some of the finest players ever to wear the winged helmet: Tom Harmon, Forest Evashevski, Bob Westfall, Albert and Alvin Wistert, Pete and Bump Elliott, Chappuis and Jack Weisenburger, to name just a few. Only two of his ten teams finished lower than second place. His .805 winning percentage is second in school history to Yost's. He stepped down as coach after leading his 1947 team to an undefeated season and the Rose Bowl, but he left his successor, Bennie Oosterbaan, a juggernaut: The Wolverines won the national championship the following season. For all his football success, however, Crisler said he was most proud that his former players earned their degrees and went on to become successful citizens, husbands, and fathers.

He would have a lasting impact on college football as Michigan's athletic director. His penchant for keeping the game honorable and safe influenced the NCAA Rules Committee for thirty-five years. During that period the committee added restrictions on cleats and various types of hard pads, introduced certification of helmet quality, and made mandatory the use of mouth guards. He also pushed for rule changes that would ensure the safety of players.

For his many contributions as player, coach, and athletic director, the Football Writers Association of America paid him the ultimate compliment when he retired as Michigan athletic director in 1968: It named him Coach of the Year. He had not coached a game in more than two decades.

Bo Schembechler

It wasn't a Big Ten championship or a Rose Bowl victory that convinced Bo Schembechler that he was a success as Michigan football coach. It was the words of one of his predecessors, former Michigan All-American Bennie Oosterbaan.

"I remember when he told me, 'Bo, you've been good for Michigan.' That meant I'd made it, that Bennie said that to me," Schembechler recalled at a memorial service for Oosterbaan in 1990.

Oosterbaan wasn't the only one who thought so, not by a long shot. Schembechler had retired a year earlier as the winningest coach in school history, compiling a 194–48–5 record. Thirteen of his twenty-one teams won or tied for Big Ten championships, and he guided seventeen teams to bowl games. Maybe most impressive of all, in twenty-seven years of coaching, including six at Miami of Ohio, he never had a losing season.

Throughout his tenure as head coach, Schembechler was admired and adored by most of his players, and he always considered that his legacy. One of his former players once recalled that Schembechler kept repeating the same message to his players, that ten years down the road they would not look back on the games, the practices, or the disciplines, but at the people with whom they played.

And they would forever remember the man who coached them, the man who expected and demanded their best, even when they didn't believe it was possible.

"His leadership ability was appealing from the beginning," said Garvie Craw, a fullback on Schembechler's first Michigan

team. "It was a different style. He led by example. He worked harder than anyone on the field. Sometimes I'd be up early in the morning, and I'd see his car there. It would be 11:30 at night, and he'd be there. He demanded that of his staff and his players. He set the tone."

Schembechler hadn't been Michigan athletic director Don Canham's first choice to succeed Bump Elliott as head coach following the 1968 season. Canham first offered the job to Penn State's Joe Paterno, who turned him down rather than leave his team right before its bowl game. Several days later, Canham called Paterno again, this time to ask him if he knew anything about the coach at Miami of Ohio, a guy named Schembechler. Paterno didn't, but he recalled a conversation he'd had with Ohio State's Woody Hayes, who had told him he considered Schembechler to be one of the young coaches who was ready for a big-time job. Paterno passed along that recommendation. The rest is history.

The energetic and intense Schembechler was a dramatic change from the easygoing Bump Elliott. Those who couldn't stomach the new coach left the team. Those who stayed . . . became champions. "We were all in a little bit of shock by how Bo came in and grabbed us all by the shoulders and shook us," former Michigan All-American Dan Dierdorf recalled. "He pushed us to try harder, work harder, and play harder. That was the magic of Bo, and it worked. We instantly gained respect for him, and we started winning. You can do a lot when you win. I went to UM to play for Bump, but we got to see before anyone else the greatness of Bo."

Coach Bo Schembechler has a word with Glenn Doughty (22) during Michigan's 24–12 win against Ohio State in 1969.
(Ann Arbor News)

He's All Heart

Bo Schembechler's players regularly expressed amazement at their head coach's energy, intensity, and work ethic. Nothing, it seemed, could slow him down. Nothing . . . except his heart.

The condition of Schembechler's heart would be an issue virtually throughout his career as Michigan coach. He suffered a heart attack the night before the 1970 Rose Bowl game. He had open-heart surgery twice, once in the spring of 1976 and again in December 1987. The second surgery, to perform a quadruple bypass, kept Schembechler from coaching in the 1988 Hall of Fame Bowl against Alabama.

"Medical science gets better as I get older, so, chances are, I will live a long life," Schembechler said in a January 1988 interview. "I have no fear. Going into the operation? You bet your life I did."

Schembechler made it clear during the same interview that he had no intention of stepping down as Michigan coach: "There is no change in my future. I always plan to coach. If you have a job you don't like and had a couple of these operations, it gives you a legitimate opportunity to quit. But you'd be a damn fool to think I'd be happy picking up the golf clubs and chasing around Florida. That sounds good to some, but not to me."

He coached two more seasons before stepping down following the 1990 Rose Bowl.

Hayes might have reconsidered that recommendation if he knew what his protégé—Schembechler had played and coached under Hayes—had in store for him. His 1969 Ohio State team, the defending national champion, was considered such a powerhouse that sportswriters joked that the Buckeyes should play the Minnesota Vikings rather than Michigan. The Wolverines had other ideas, however, and in one of the greatest upsets in college football history, they stunned the Buckeyes, 24–12, at Michigan Stadium.

That game, arguably the most important ever played by a Michigan football team, restored the program to what Yost would have said was its proper place among college football's elite. And it has remained there. Although other top programs have struggled through rebuilding and losing seasons, Michigan's excellence has remained a constant.

"Obviously, that ['69 Ohio State] game was a turning point," said Fritz Seyferth, who played and coached under Schembechler. "[But] let's understand that many of these kids were here because of the tradition. That didn't start with Bo. But there had been a drought of the excellence that people expected. Bo gave a sign that things were changing. He started what has been maintained."

In an editorial published the day after Schembechler coached for the last time in the 1990 Rose Bowl (a 17–10 loss to Southern Cal), the *Ann Arbor News* wrote: "Bo may have coached his last game Monday, but he isn't retiring. Legends don't retire. Schembechler's legacy will affect the way Michigan plays football for years to come. He has set a tradition . . . and the payoff is admiration and respect from the players he's coached . . . and gratitude from Michigan fans from coast to coast. Part of Michigan's greatness is because of Bo Schembechler."

Yost with the Most

The 1901 Point-a-Minute Team

T he day he arrived in Ann Arbor in 1901, new University of Michigan football coach Fielding H. Yost promised that his team would not lose a game.

It was the sort of prediction that today almost certainly would wind up on a bulletin board in an opponent's locker room, but Yost was nothing if not confident and cocky.

He also was prophetic. His first five teams combined to produce a 55–1–1 record and earned the nickname "Point-a-Minute" because they were so prolific offensively. They scored 2,821 points to the opposition's 42. They played fifty-six games without a loss and had winning streaks of twenty-nine and twenty-six games, still the longest in school history.

"No other coach and no other football team ever so dominated their era as Fielding H. Yost and the Michigan teams for 1901–05," Yost biographer John Behee wrote.

And none of Yost's teams did more to create and define Michigan's tradition of football excellence than his 1901 team, which started it all.

That team finished 11–0 and outscored opponents, 550–0. Several games were cut short because an opponent conceded— which rules allowed at the time—so the Wolverines actually averaged more than a point a minute. Michigan wrapped up the season with a 49–0 win against Stanford in the first Rose Bowl. Michigan and Harvard were recognized that season as national champions.

Michigan was Yost's fifth coaching stop in as many years. He would never coach anywhere else. His twenty-five Michigan teams won 196 games. Thirteen of them were unbeaten.

Yost was a West Virginia native who had attended Ohio Normal College and the University of West Virginia Law School. As a rookie coach in 1897, he led Ohio Wesleyan to its only win against Ohio State and a tie against Michigan. Wanting to see the country, he moved to Nebraska and then to Kansas, and he coached both teams to Missouri Valley championships. Missouri tried to hire Yost in 1890, but he moved to California. There, he coached the Stanford freshmen, Lowell High School of San Francisco, San Jose Teachers College, and a team called California Ukiah—all in the same season.

Stanford officials liked Yost, but, following a common practice at the time, they decided at the end of the 1900 season to hire only alumni to coach their teams. So, out of a job in December 1900, Yost wrote to the University of Illinois. There were no openings there, but the Illinois manager of athletics passed Yost's letter along to his Michigan counterpart, Charles Baird. Michigan sought to hire a coach to replace Langdon "Biff" Lee, who finished 7–2–1 in 1900 but had lost to rival Chicago and finished fifth in the Western Conference.

Baird immediately wrote to Yost: "Our people are greatly roused up over the defeats of the past two years, and a great effort will be made." Baird offered Yost free room and board and a $2,300 salary—the same amount a full professor earned. Yost responded by sending a fifty-pound package containing newspaper clippings and reference letters.

Arriving by cross-country train in Ann Arbor, Yost was met at the depot by Baird, who introduced himself and immediately asked whether Yost really had coached four teams during the same season while he was in California, as he claimed in his résumé. Yost thought about it for a moment, then counted the teams on the fingers of one hand. No, he admitted, the number actually was five. He'd forgotten he'd helped out with the Stanford varsity team, too.

One of Yost's star players at San Jose Teachers College was Willie Heston, who, by the time Yost arrived in Ann Arbor, was teaching school in California. Yost wrote to Heston, asking him to come to Michigan. Heston, who hailed from Grants Pass, Oregon, initially refused, but he changed his mind and eventually purchased the unused half of a round-trip train ticket from San Francisco to Toledo for $25 and came east. Arriving unannounced, Heston wandered the Michigan campus for several hours until a delighted Yost spotted him.

Reports were that Heston was so fast that he could easily win match races against Archie Hahn, who won three gold medals in sprint events in the 1904 Olympics. Heston also had great feet. He was so good that Yost created a new position for him, the better to get him the ball more quickly. Heston lined up a few yards behind the line of scrimmage and became the game's first tailback. Heston scored seventy-two touchdowns in thirty-six games at Michigan, including a team-high twenty during the 1901 season. He would earn All-America honors in 1903 and 1904.

Yost developed a play for Heston, called "Old 83," that became the most famous of its day. The Wolverines would line up strong to the right side. Then, the quarterback would get the snap from center and fake a handoff to the fullback, who ran around the right side with the whole line blocking for him. Just as the pileup started, the quarterback would hand the ball to Heston, who would race downfield on the left side.

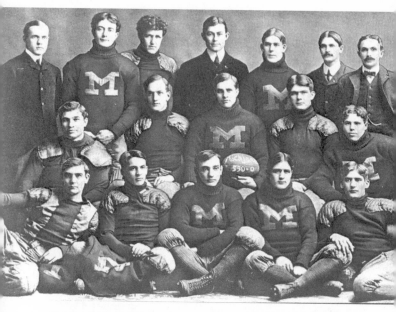

Fielding H. Yost's "Point-a-Minute" 1901 football team. Yost is in the center in the back row. The team's two offensive stars are in the middle row. Neil Snow is second from left. Willie Heston is the player on the right.
(Bentley Historical Library)

The Wolverines ran the play for the first time in the 1902 Rose Bowl. It reportedly was the first bootleg in college football history.

The other star of the 1901 team—and its only All-American—was Neil Snow, who finished second to Heston that season with nineteen touchdowns. Snow, of Detroit, earned ten letters while at Michigan playing football and baseball and running track. Snow already had played three seasons at Michigan when Yost arrived, but the coach, recognizing Snow's abilities, converted him from end to fullback, a much more important position in a running offense.

A Different Game

College football as it was played a century ago was considerably different than it is today. Here are some of the 1901 rules:

- The field was 110 yards long.
- Games lasted seventy minutes, with two thirty-five-minute halves, but games could be and often were shortened.
- Players played both offense and defense, and if a player left for a substitute, he could not return to the game.
- No forward passing was permitted.
- Tackles and guards were allowed to run the ball.
- Three downs were allowed to gain 5 yards for a first down.
- Touchdowns and field goals each counted five points. Extra points were worth one point. No two-point conversions were allowed.
- After a touchdown the scoring team received the kickoff, which helps to explain why the scores of games were so lopsided.

From the beginning Yost instilled in quarterback Harrison "Boss" Weeks the urgency of his lightning-fast offense. Weeks would call signals while he was still under the pile from the previous play. If a player did not get up quickly enough to suit Yost, the coach would holler at him from the sideline, "Are you just a spectator? Hurry up! Hurry up!"

That reportedly is how Yost earned his nickname "Hurry-Up Yost."

Heston was asked decades later to describe Yost's style and tactical impact on the game. He wrote: "He brought to Michigan an entirely new brand of football, not known in the

Big Ten or the Middle West. Particularly, that was true of his offense. Speed and more speed was continuously emphasized."

The Wolverines opened September 28 with a 50–0 win against Albion before an enthusiastic crowd of 2,000 at Regents Field. Captain Hugh White scored three of Michigan's nine touchdowns. Heston made his debut in the second half and scored a touchdown.

Case, a Cleveland school, was next on the schedule, but the game was nearly cancelled because of an argument about the officials. Once that was resolved, the Wolverines rolled to a 57–0 win. Heston scored four touchdowns, all in the second half. Case finished with just one first down.

Michigan opened Western Conference play the following weekend with a 33–0 win against Indiana. The game was played in a constant drizzle that reduced Regents Field to a quagmire. That didn't stop Weeks from delivering a sensational 75-yard run to set up Michigan's third touchdown.

Heston didn't start at first because Yost believed that the Michigan seniors should be given the first shot at playing time. Heston made his debut in the second half against Albion and scored a touchdown. He didn't start in the next game, either. Minutes into the third game against Indiana, fans in the bleachers began to chant: "We want Heston."

The chant continued, and Yost finally turned to Heston and said, "Well, go in there and show them what you can do." Walter Shaw, the starter who played left halfback the year before, walked off the field and reportedly never put his football uniform on again.

The Wolverines' shutout string nearly came to an end during the second half of the October 19 game against Northwestern. The Wildcats drove to the Michigan 2 yard line in the second half, but the Wolverines held on downs.

Michigan claimed its biggest win of the season October 26, rolling over Buffalo, 128–0. Buffalo came to Ann Arbor fresh off a win against Eastern power Columbia, but it was no match for the Wolverines, who scored twenty-two touchdowns, including five by Albert Herrnstein. Playing time in the second half was reduced from thirty-five to twenty minutes.

Dad Gregory, the team's center, complained at one point that every one on the team had scored a touchdown in the game except him. Later, as the Wolverines closed in again on the goal line, Weeks signaled for Gregory to line up in the backfield and promised to hand him the ball. Gregory plowed through the line and dove into the end zone, yelling, "I'm over! I'm over!" However, Weeks played a trick on the play, pulling the ball away at the last second so that Gregory was not awarded the touchdown.

During the game a Buffalo substitute staggered to the Michigan bench. "Son, you're on the wrong side," Yost informed him. "Oh, no, I ain't," the player replied, and he sat down.

Buffalo students refused to believe the score as it was printed in newspapers. They did only after the Buffalo players returned to campus and confirmed what had happened.

The Wolverines next faced Carlisle and its legendary coach, Glen "Pop" Warner, at Detroit's Bennett Park (later Tiger Stadium). More than 8,000 fans watched Michigan post a 22–0 win.

Ohio State, not yet a member of the Western Conference, gave Michigan its toughest game of the season before losing 21–0 in Columbus. Neil Snow scored two touchdowns, and White and Heston each added one. The Buckeyes drove deep into Michigan territory in the second half but were turned back.

Michigan celebrated Alumni Day (now called homecoming) with a 22–0 win against its biggest rival, Chicago, coached by Amos Alonzo Stagg. The Maroons crossed midfield just once during the game.

The November 23 home finale was played in muddy, slippery conditions, but the Wolverines still managed fifteen touchdowns in an 89–0 win against Beloit. Herrnstein scored six touchdowns, including one on a 60-yard run.

Michigan crushed defending Western Conference champion Iowa, 50–0, in a game played on a cold Thanksgiving Day in front of a capacity crowd of 10,000 at Chicago's West Side Park. Snow cleared from the field was piled high along the sidelines. Bruce Shorts and Heston each scored four touchdowns.

The season was finished, but the Wolverines weren't. Yost agreed to play a postseason game on New Year's Day against his former Stanford team.

The first Rose Bowl game was the project of the Tournament of Roses organization in Pasadena, California. Each year, the city sponsored a New Year's festival in which townspeople decorated their carriages, buggies, and horses with roses and other flowers and held a parade. The festival had grown to the point where the committee wanted to add a sports attraction to grab national attention. After deciding on a football game, committee members invited Michigan, the best team in the country, to play Stanford, the best team in the West, in a "Tournament of Roses" football game.

The game gave the Michigan team a chance to leave the cold for a few days. When the team boarded the train for the long ride west, it was ten degrees below zero in Ann Arbor. The temperature in southern California was eighty-five degrees when the Wolverines arrived.

The Wolverines practiced long and hard once they arrived. Yost wanted to make sure his players still had their stamina after a month layoff, because he worried that the heat would wear his boys down.

Yost was concerned enough about the heat that he tried to persuade Stanford coach C. M. Fickert to shorten each of the scheduled thirty-five-minute halves by ten minutes. Fickert replied: "We can't do that Mr. Yost. We have sold a great many tickets for the game, and [the spectators] are entitled to see two full halves." For the moment, anyway, the subject was dropped.

On New Year's morning, Michigan players participated in the Rose Parade. Outfitted in new uniforms, the players waved colorful Michigan banners and rode in a large carriage. The city was a riot of color, mostly blue and gold, which by a strange coincidence had been adopted as the year's official colors of the tournament. Blue-and-gold pennants were everywhere. The color combination so closely resembled Michigan's colors that some of the Stanford faithful, a bit miffed by what they thought was a show of support for their opponents, began to tear down the banners and streamers.

The Tournament of Roses East–West Game was played on the campus of Throop Polytechnic Institute, now known as the California Institute of Technology. Although the Pasadena stadium had only about 1,000 seats, an estimated 8,500 patrons forced their way into Tournament Park to watch the game. Many who waited and had reserved seats entered the bleachers only to find their seats taken by fans who had sneaked in over the fence. Many ticket holders and some without them watched the game standing along the sides of the playing field.

Stanford entered the game with a 3–1–2 record—the only loss was 2–0 to rival California—but it was still the underdog because it had not faced a schedule as difficult as Michigan's.

Weeks, Shorts, Snow, Heston, Herrnstein

TACKLE-BACK-RIGHT PLAY.

Quarterback Harrison "Boss" Weeks hands the ball to Neil Snow, who busts into the end zone for one of his five touchdowns in Michigan's 49–0 win against Stanford in the 1902 Rose Bowl. *(Bentley Historical Library)*

Only two of Stanford's games were played against college football teams. The other four were played against the Olympic and Reliance football clubs. Stanford had played each club team twice.

The first twenty-two minutes of the scoreless game were well played. Michigan lined up in punt formation at the Stanford 29. Instead, Yost ran a fake using his new play, "Old 83." The Michigan players swung out to the right, and the full-back appeared to be running right with the football. Then, just as the pileup started, Heston took a handoff and ran around the left side. He was finally tackled when he reached the Stanford 8 yard line. Four plays later, Snow bulled into the end zone for a 5–0 lead. Michigan soon scored two more times in building a 17–0 half-time lead.

In the second half the Stanford defense wilted in the face of Michigan's three-pronged running attack. Snow, the player of the game, finished with 107 yards and five touchdowns. Heston added 170 yards on eighteen carries, and Herrnstein chipped in with 97 yards and a touchdown. Meanwhile, end Ev Sweeley kicked four field goals and punted twenty-one times for a 38.9 average.

At one point during the second half, Stanford's Fickert approached Yost and asked if he would agree to cancel the remainder of the game, claiming that he could not field eleven healthy players. Remembering the earlier conversation about the heat, Yost replied: "We can't do that. All of these people who have bought seats to see this game are entitled to see two full thirty-five-minute halves." Fickert countered: "Ninety-five percent of this crowd are Stanford fans, and I think they feel they have seen enough and would like to go home."

Finally, with eight minutes remaining, Stanford captain Ralph Fisher approached his Michigan counterpart, White, with the offer: "If you are willing, we are ready to quit." The Wolverines accepted. Using modern scoring rules, the final score would have been 55–0.

Because the game had not been competitive and because of problems with the stampeding crowd that had crammed into the stadium, football fell out of favor with the Tournament of Roses officials, even though they had realized a profit of $3,161.86 on the game. A year later, Tournament Park instead hosted a polo match. Inspired by the popularity of the literary classic *Ben Hur*, Roman-style chariot races were featured from 1904–15.

Responding to public demand, the association reinstated football at Tournament Park in 1916. Seven years later, the new Rose Bowl Stadium hosted its first Rose Bowl game. A Western Conference/Big Ten team did not return to Pasadena until 1920. Michigan would not play there again until 1948.

Yost would coach twenty-four more seasons and finish with 165 victories to his credit. His teams won ten conference championships, and twenty of his players earned All-American honors. And, although each of his teams contributed to Michigan's tradition of excellence, it was the 1901 team that started it and defined it.

That tradition would one day inspire the legendary sportswriter Grantland Rice to wax poetic:

> *I remember the stand at Thermopylae*
> *The Greek Guard made one day;*
> *I remember the legions that Caesar used*
> *To shatter the Gallic sway;*
> *And I remember across the years*
> *Two banners that crowned the crest*
> *When Yale was king of the conquered East,*
> *And Michigan ruled the West.*
>
> *At night in my humble den I dream*
> *Of the glories that used to be —*
> *Of Hannibal taking the Alpine trail,*
> *Of Drake on the open sea.*
> *And then I wander the ancient ways*
> *To a dream I love the best,*
> *When Yale was king of the conquered East,*
> *And Michigan ruled the West.*

The 1901 Season

Michigan 50, Albion 0: Captain Hugh White scores three of the Wolverines' nine touchdowns before a crowd of 2,000 at Regents Field. Star tailback Willie Heston makes his debut in the second half and scores a touchdown.

Michigan 57, Case 0: After the game is nearly canceled because of an argument about one of the officials, Heston scores four touchdowns, all in the second half. Case gains just one first down.

Michigan 33, Indiana 0: The first Western Conference game is played in a constant drizzle that reduces Regents Field to a quagmire. Still, quarterback Harrison "Boss" Weeks delivers a sensational 75-yard run to set up Michigan's third touchdown.

Michigan 29, Northwestern 0: The Wolverines' streak nearly comes to an end in the second half, when the Wildcats drive to Michigan's 2 yard line. The Wolverines hold there on downs.

Michigan 128, Buffalo 0: Though fresh off a win against Eastern power Columbia, Buffalo is no match for the Wolverines. Michigan scores twenty-two touchdowns, including five by Albert Herrnstein. Playing time in the second half is reduced from thirty-five to twenty minutes.

Michigan 22, Carlisle 0: The game, played before 6,000 fans at Detroit's Bennett Park, features two of the game's legendary coaches, Michigan's Fielding Yost and Carlisle's Glen "Pop" Warner.

Michigan 21, Ohio State 0: Neil Snow scores two touchdowns and White and Heston each score one against Ohio State, which is not yet a member of the conference. The Buckeyes drive deep into Michigan territory in the second half but are turned back.

Michigan 22, Chicago 0: The Wolverines celebrate Alumni Day (now homecoming) with a win against archrival Chicago, coached by Amos Alonzo Stagg. The Maroons cross midfield just once.

Michigan 89, Beloit 0: In the home finale played on a muddy field, the Wolverines score fifteen touchdowns. Herrnstein scores six of them, including one on a 60-yard run.

Michigan 50, Iowa 0: On Thanksgiving Day in front of a capacity crowd in Chicago's West Side Park, the Wolverines crush the defending conference champions on the strength of four touchdowns apiece by Bruce Shorts and Heston.

Michigan 49, Stanford 0: Snow scored five touchdowns—a Rose Bowl record that still stands—in the first Rose Bowl. Michigan gained 527 yards to Stanford's 67.

Building Michigan Stadium

Yost Wanted a Bigger "Big House"

I magine if Michigan Stadium, nicknamed "The Big House," was bigger. Significantly bigger.

Fielding H. Yost, who during two decades as University of Michigan athletic director built athletic facilities that were second to none, imagined just that. From the moment it was opened in 1927, Michigan Stadium has, almost exclusively, been the largest college-owned stadium in the nation. The stadium was expanded six times during the twentieth century—and almost certainly will be again in the new millennium—but never in quite the way Yost envisioned it.

"When Yost built the stadium, he said it should be built for 300,000 fans," former Michigan athletic director Don Canham told the *Ann Arbor News* in a 1990 interview. "He saw the need for seats for 500,000 people." Canham did point out, however, that Yost made his proposals in the years before professional football and television began to steal away potential paying customers.

In a book commemorating the sixtieth anniversary of the stadium in 1987, Michigan alumnus Bob Rosiek wrote that one of Yost's proposals for the new stadium called for an upper deck that would increase stadium capacity to 150,000 or more.

Although the stadium design approved by the university's Board of Regents called for only half that many permanent seats, Yost ordered the stadium constructed with double concrete footings. Yost's explanation: The footings provided a solid foundation in an area surrounded by quicksand and a high water table. But the footings also made possible the addition of a second deck.

Determined to see the new stadium built according to his vision and not the limited views of others, Yost would butt heads with the university's faculty and Regents, as well as many people in the Ann Arbor community, as he planned the stadium and oversaw its construction. Through his dogged perseverance, he would make his dream a reality.

A faculty committee appointed by the Regents to study the university's intramural, physical education, and intercollegiate athletic programs had recommended building a new stadium, but with a capacity for no more than 60,000 spectators. Many in the Ann Arbor community believed that anything larger would injure the university academically, intellectually, and socially. As one faculty member noted at the time: "The building of a new stadium would be a permanent and undeniable concession—set in concrete for years to come—to the notion that college is nothing more than a Roman holiday."

Yost ignored the committee's recommendation, but he did follow its instructions to build a stadium "of the utmost simplicity, with no attempt made to give it the form of a monument or memorial." Three-quarters of the rectangular stadium was built below ground level, and when it opened in 1927, it had 72,000 permanent seats. A wide concrete concourse around the rim of the stadium allowed for temporary bleachers, and a sellout crowd of 84,401 attended the dedication game on October 22, 1927. The Wolverines treated spectators to a 21–0 victory over Ohio State that afternoon.

"Yost had great vision," said the late Cliff Keen, who came to Michigan as wrestling coach in 1925. "He was ridiculed for thinking so big, but he went with his ideas anyway. There was all kinds of talk at the time that a stadium that large would be a monstrosity. The idea of a second deck would have sounded ridiculous at the time."

Though Michigan teams had played games in Ann Arbor since 1883, the Wolverines did not have a field to call their own until ten years later. Following a successful season in 1890, the Regents authorized $3,000 for the purchase of a tract of land along South State Street (where Schembechler Hall sits today). A year later, the Regents approved an additional $5,000 to improve drainage and put the field into shape. On October 7, 1893, Michigan played on a permanent home site for the first time, defeating the Detroit Athletic Club, 6–0.

The new home was named Regents Field. It opened with a single wooden bleacher section that held 400 people, but many more fans would show up for the games. The original bleachers burned down in 1895, and the Regents ordered the construction of covered stands the following year. That doubled the seating capacity, but it still fell far short of meeting demand. Many times, temporary seats were erected to accommodate as many as 17,000 spectators.

In 1902 Detroit native Dexter M. Ferry donated twenty-one acres of land that stretched west from South State Street to the university. The donation united the land that is now the athletic campus. In recognition of the gift, the Regents renamed the entire complex Ferry Field. By then, Yost was head football coach, and his powerful Michigan teams were extremely popular. The Wolverines needed a new home, and the Regents approved the construction of a new Ferry Field that sat where the university's outdoor track is now.

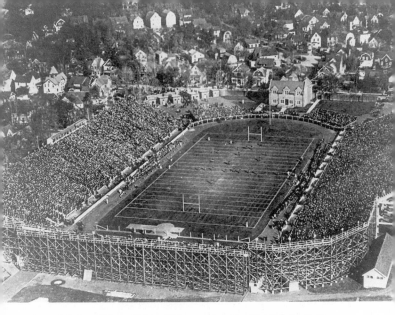

An aerial view of Ferry Field, which served as the Michigan football team's home from 1906–26 (Bentley Historical Library)

Unlike the old field, which also was home to the baseball and track teams, the new Ferry Field was designed for the sole use of the football team—and only on game days. The stadium opened in 1906 with a seating capacity of 18,000, and it boasted a press box to facilitate growing media interest in the team. Fans paid $1.00 for a ticket. Students paid 50 cents—conference rules prohibited schools from charging any more than that.

Yost pushed for more seats. In 1921, when he took on the additional duties of athletic director, the Regents granted him permission to erect temporary wooden bleachers at both ends of the stadium. That pushed the seating capacity to 40,000. Still, Yost was not satisfied.

Because of the growing popularity of college football across the country, a number of schools built new stadiums during the early part of the 1920s. Michigan had the honor of being the opponent in dedication games for new stadiums at Vanderbilt, Ohio State, Michigan State, and Illinois. Conference rivals Minnesota, Northwestern, and Purdue also had new stadiums. Yost began to plan for a stadium that would surpass all the others.

In late October 1925, the university's Board in Control of Intercollegiate Athletics gave its general approval to a building plan submitted by Yost, "which contains as its chief item the building of a stadium that will seat approximately 70,000, and which will be capable of further enlargements, if necessary." Instead of rubber stamping the recommendation, the Regents appointed the faculty study committee to "inquire into the whole athletic situation." Among its many responsibilities, the committee was instructed to form "a very definite expression of opinion on the subject of a [new] stadium."

The committee concluded that the stands at Ferry Field were sufficient for some games but not large enough to take care of the crowds that poured into Ann Arbor to witness the two or three "big games" on the schedule each year. In its report the committee wrote: "In our opinion, if the modern status of intercollegiate athletic competition is to be continued, the erection of a stadium with a greatly increased seating capacity is not only logical but probably necessary."

But the committee's vision of a new stadium clearly was much less grandiose than Yost's was. It recommended a seating capacity of not more than 60,000. It did not want the stadium to possess any particular sentimental qualities, nor did it want the stadium to be a memorial of any kind. It further wrote: "In view of these facts, it seems to us that an elaborate, impressive, and costly stadium would be a useless waste of money, at once inappropriate and in exceedingly bad taste.

Why One?

ince Michigan Stadium was expanded in 1956 to seat more than 100,000, the official capacity of college football's largest stadium has always ended in "01." Why the additional seat? The tradition began—and continues—as a way to honor Fritz Crisler, then Michigan's director of athletics. Michigan Stadium played host to more than 100,000 spectators for the first time on October 6, 1956, when Michigan State defeated Michigan, 9–0.

There is no cause to build anything other than the simplest and most economical stadium, which will accommodate an adequate number of spectators and give them a clear and unobstructed view."

The committee also offered two interesting observations, both of which still hold true. First, it foresaw that intercollegiate football would become the main source of financial support for other athletic activities. Second, it warned that universities had to stand firm against the excesses of alumni and fans. The committee wrote: "One of the most serious difficulties in intercollegiate football at this present time is the insistence of alumni upon winning teams. Efforts must be made to keep alumni opinion sane and conservative in matters of athletic policy, and, furthermore, to develop among alumni an interest in phases of university activity other than the purely athletic."

Having read the report, Yost responded to the Regents with a letter that, for all intents and purposes, criticized the committee's lack of vision regarding the construction of athletic facilities, particularly a stadium. He wrote: "To argue against the erection of a new stadium is to . . . maintain that the whole present day attitude toward athletics is unsound and open to objection."

Yost was determined to work around the committee and, if need be, the Regents. Instead of mounting a direct attack, Yost included the stadium proposal in a long list of improvements designed to benefit "Athletics for All," a hot movement in the 1920s. Halfway down his ten-point list of immediate and pressing needs to meet this new demand, Yost buried "Increased seating capacity for football stands," though it almost certainly was the item he cared most passionately about.

The committee was adamant in its opposition to any plan involving the sale of bonds that carried the privilege of preferred stadium seating, but Yost already had moved ahead with a plan to do just that. The athletic department sold 3,000 tax-exempt bonds for $500 (about $5,000 in today's dollars). The sale raised $1.5 million. Buyers earned 3 percent interest annually, and Yost promised to pay off the bonds over the next twenty years. Because of the Great Depression, not a penny was paid on the bonds from 1931–36. The bonds were completely retired in October 1947.

There was added incentive to purchase a bond: It also earned fans the right to purchase season tickets at midfield for ten years, beginning in 1927. In a brochure sent to prospective investors, Yost made it clear that those who didn't buy bonds risked missing games entirely. "There will be no justifiable complaint if one finds himself outside of the stadium on the day of the game, since the opportunity to assure one's self of good tickets was passed up when available," he wrote.

The *Ann Arbor Times News* pointed out in a story about

Michigan athletic director Fielding H. Yost poses at the new Michigan Stadium in 1927. (Bentley Historical Library)

the stadium the day before the dedication game that Michigan was the first and only school in the country that had built a stadium without asking for donations from alumni or financial assistance from the state. The cost of the stadium was $1,124,000, which included $100,000 for drainage, $200,000 for excavation, $500,000 for construction, $30,000 for plumbing, $25,000 for grading, $10,000 for heating and ventilation, and $9,000 for lighting. The cost also included the $250,000 Yost paid to acquire the forty-five acres of land on which the stadium would sit.

The construction of the stadium was complicated by the fact that a lake and a spring, which for years had fed the university's water needs, were located under the property. Much of the surface resembled quicksand. The moist surface engulfed a crane during the excavation stage of the project. According to legend, the crane remains under the stadium to this day. The excavation for the bowl necessitated the digging of 260,000 cubic yards of earth. It was a cut-and-fill proposition: The dirt dug out of the hole was used to grade the area around the outside of the stadium.

Workers placed 800 concrete footings, using 440 tons of reinforcing steel and 31,000 square feet of wire mesh. Killins Gravel of Ann Arbor placed a full-page advertisement in a special stadium section published October 21, 1927 by the *Ann Arbor Times News*, noting that it had provided the 25,000 tons of washed gravel that was used.

Fashioned after the Yale Bowl, the stadium featured forty-four sections and seventy-two rows. The original seats consisted of 22 miles of California redwood, and the 360-foot by 160-foot grass field included the planting of one four-leaf clover. The press box had seating for 270 sportswriters and three sound-proof booths for radio broadcasts. The dedication game against Ohio State was broadcast by WWJ radio of Detroit and WEAO of Columbus, Ohio. Envisioning even more in the future, Yost ordered that eight large conduits be built in the cement to handle the wiring necessary for electronic media.

Construction took a little more than a year. Ground was broken on September 15, 1926, and the last of the work was done on October 1, 1927—the same day the Wolverines opened the stadium with a game against Ohio Wesleyan.

Ann Arbor native Kip Taylor caught a 28-yard pass from Louis Gilbert for the first touchdown ever scored in the stadium, and the Wolverines went on to post a 33–0 win in that first game. The paid attendance for the opener was 17,483, but high school students from all over the state were invited as

Cover of the program from the Michigan Stadium dedication game, played October 22, 1927, against Ohio State. The Wolverines won, 21–0. (Bentley Historical Library)

guests of the university, and they swelled the attendance to close to 50,000. A week later, 27,864 watched as Michigan posted a 21–0 win against Michigan State.

The stadium was not officially dedicated until October 22, when Ohio State paid a visit. Yost explained the decision to wait three weeks: "I can think of nothing that expresses Michigan's regard for Ohio State more tangibly . . . than the formal opening of our new stadium. When a man is married, he invariably invites his best friend to be his best man. When he accomplishes something exceptionally worthwhile, it is his closest friend who is first with congratulations. And so it followed that, when we planned the formal opening of the new stadium, we should single out Ohio to meet us on the gridiron."

The guest speakers at the dedication included the governors of both states, Michigan's Fred W. Green and Ohio's Vic Donahey, and the presidents of both universities, UM's Clarence C. Little and Ohio State's George W. Rightmire.

If there were any hard feelings left over from the wrangling among Yost, the Regents, and members of the faculty, they apparently were forgiven—or at least temporarily forgotten—in the euphoria over the opening of the new stadium. Little, the university president, told the capacity crowd: "I hope the true significance of this magnificent new structure may be felt by all who sit here or play here. For the University of Michigan, its faculty, students, and alumni, I can say sincerely that [the stadium] is not a monument to mere pride nor to the commercial side of modern college sports. It is a place to play games, and a place where our friends may join us as competitors and spectators. We believe in athletics, and in athletics for all."

The Buckeyes had revenge on their minds that afternoon. Five years earlier, the Wolverines had spoiled the dedication of Ohio Stadium with a 19–0 victory. The 1926 game at Ohio Stadium was one of the classics of the series. The Wolverines won, 17–16, handing the Buckeyes their only loss of the season.

The 1927 dedication game was not a classic in the grand sense, but it did feature classic performances by two Wolverines. Bennie Oosterbaan, an All-American, threw three passes in the game, all to halfback Louis Gilbert. All three passes went for touchdowns. Statistically, it was a strange game. Subtract the three touchdown plays, and Michigan finished with just 93 total yards. Ohio State had a decisive advantage in first downs (10–4) and total yards (191–163).

In an editorial published the day before the dedication game, the *Ann Arbor Times News* applauded the university for its vision in building the new stadium. Noting that proceeds from the use of the stadium would be used for a physical education program at the university, the newspaper praised the building of the stadium as yet another commitment to excellence in the community. "Is it not gratifying to look down into that bowl and realize that it is not a product of philanthropy or taxation . . ., but that it is a contribution by intercollegiate football to the cause of physical development and wholesome, healthy living?" the newspaper wrote. "Is it not gratifying, likewise, to know that the stadium is not a monument to some-

An aerial view of Michigan Stadium (Ann Arbor News)

thing that is dead and gone, but rather a symbol of life and youth?"

Ironically, the editorial did not mention Yost, who had had to cajole and coerce university officials to build the stadium in the first place.

The seating capacity of Michigan Stadium was increased to 97,239 in 1949, when permanent steel bleachers replaced the wooden ones. Engineering reports confirmed then that the footings were so deep they could easily support a second deck.

Canham said that although an upper deck often was a

Michigan Stadium Timeline

1927: Michigan Stadium opens with seventy permanent rows to seat 72,000 fans. Additional wooden bleachers increase capacity to 84,401.

1930: Electronic scoreboards are erected at both ends of the stadium. Michigan Stadium is the first to use them to keep official time.

1949: Permanent steel bleachers are constructed to replace the wooden bleachers, raising capacity to 97,239.

1956: Capacity is increased again, this time to 101,001. Also included in this expansion is the construction of a $700,000 press box.

1969: At a cost of $250,000, 88,285 feet of Tartan Turf is installed, replacing the stadium's grass field. The Wolverines will play on artificial turf fields through 1990.

1973: Capacity is increased to 101,701, as box seats and railings are removed from the first few rows and replaced with bleacher seats.

1991: Grass is back, as 87,000 feet of Prescription Athletic Turf is installed. In addition the playing surface is lowered nearly 4 feet to facilitate better sightlines for those seated in the lower rows. The entire project costs $2.25 million.

1992: Capacity is increased to 102,501 with the addition of a ninety-second row of bleachers.

1998: The stadium undergoes renovations that add 5,000 new seats and two video scoreboards in each end zone. Official capacity is now 107,501.

1999: Michigan breaks its own single-game attendance record, attracting 111,575 spectators for the season finale against Ohio State.

2002: School administrators decide to replace the torn-up grass field with a new synthetic surface that looks, feels, and plays like grass. The new field goes in for the 2003 season.

topic of conversation, the construction of one was never seriously considered by university athletic officials. "There was never a serious discussion of it because they never sold the seats they had," he said. "It took some doing to get a full house." Michigan did not begin to average more than 100,000 for its home dates until 1976.

Today, as in 1927, the revenue generated from games played at Michigan Stadium goes a long way in keeping the athletic department going. Certainly that much of Yost's vision was on target.

Two years before he died, a white-haired, bespectacled Yost sat in an empty Michigan Stadium reminiscing with a longtime friend, Fred Lawton. Looking out over the expanse of the place, Lawton whistled and then said, "Big, isn't it?" "Yup," Yost replied as he let loose a hearty laugh. "And the best thing about it is that people pay three dollars for every seat in it!"

The "Mad Magicians"

Fritz Crisler's 1947 Michigan Team

The nickname "Mad Magicians" fit Michigan's 1947 football team perfectly. It reflected the Wolverines' sleight-of-hand offensive repertoire, which included what *Time* magazine called "a baffling assortment of double-reverses, laterals, criss-crosses, quick hits, and spins."

One sportswriter described Michigan's backfield of halfback Bob Chappuis, wingback Chalmers "Bump" Elliott, fullback Jack Weisenburger, and quarterback Howard Yerges as "a backfield full of pervasive shadows that flit about like wraiths." Trickery and deception were so much a part of the offense that at times, as he watched from the Michigan sideline, even Michigan coach Fritz Crisler couldn't always be certain which member of his marvelous backfield had the football.

The '47 team was the legendary Crisler's last, and it was his best one. It was arguably the finest Michigan team ever. Its excellence was such that the Associated Press would take the then unprecedented step following the Wolverines' 49–0 win against Southern Cal in the 1948 Rose Bowl of holding a post-bowl poll to determine which team, Michigan or Notre Dame, deserved the national championship.

The origin of the nickname, however, is as big a mystery as its offense so often was to opposing defenses. Former team

members are not certain who coined the nickname or when it was first used. Chappuis thought some sportswriter might have used it while trying to draw a comparison between Michigan's backfield and Notre Dame's famous "Four Horsemen." Weisenburger believed that radio announcer Bill Stern might have used the nickname during his broadcast of Michigan's 1948 Rose Bowl win against Southern Cal. A 1948 university yearbook referred to the team as "Crisler's Magicians."

"I don't really know that anyone knows the answer to that one," Elliott said. "But I believe it came up later than at the time of the team. I'm not sure at the time we were ever called that. I have no idea where it came from."

By 1947 most college teams had scrapped the aging single-wing offense in favor of one that featured the T-formation, in which the quarterback lines up under center. But Crisler

preferred the single wing because size did not matter as much. That season, Michigan was a small team. The largest player weighed 220 pounds, and the offensive line averaged 182 pounds. Michigan's offense relied on skill, quickness, and ball handling.

Elliott recalled that all of Michigan's backs, both on offense and defense, at one time or another had played tailback in the single wing. That meant they could run, pass, block, and catch the ball. Also, Crisler pioneered the use of the two-platoon system: The first offensive team was the second defensive unit, and vice versa. Only Elliott and Weisenburger played both ways. "It was possible, with all those ingredients, for the 1947 team to exploit all the variations and complicated design of the famous Crisler single-wing attack," Elliott said.

An ardent admirer of Robert E. Lee's battle strategy, Crisler tried to imitate it: feinting at one point, hitting another. His system, devised over the course of several seasons, was built around nine basic delayed hits and the same number of quick hits. All eighteen could be run from seven different formations, though most were run out of the balanced and unbalanced single wing. Those plays, plus nine passing plays and some "specials" brought the total in Michigan's playbook to more than 170. The Wolverines used combinations of double-reverses, laterals, crisscrosses, quick-hitters, and spins. Ninety percent of the plays Crisler devised had at least one exchange and frequently had as many as three.

"We had to handle the ball so much and as they said, so magically," Chappuis said. "We loved to amaze people with our agility."

Chappuis recalled that the ball was touched by seven players on one particular play. Weisenburger took the ball from center, then handed it to Yerges, who then pitched it to Chappuis. He handed the ball to Bump Elliott, who handed it to one end, who then threw it to the other end. Weisenburger said the Wolverines didn't run that play often because offensive linemen were required to hold their blocks for a long time and didn't like it much.

After Michigan returned from the Rose Bowl, some students obtained film of the game and showed it at Hill Auditorium. Players were asked to narrate. Much of the time, Chappuis recalled, the players didn't know who was handling the ball and would call out the wrong names. Sometimes the deception had been so complete during the game that the cameraman shooting the film had missed the play entirely.

About 70 percent of Michigan's team was made up of former World War II servicemen whose tuition was paid by the government. They had faced worse menaces than onrushing tacklers.

Offensive tackle Bill Pritula had served with the Army engineers in the Philippines. Chappuis had been a radioman and gunner on a B-25 that flew sorties during the Italian campaign. On its twenty-first mission in early 1945, the plane was shot down. Chappuis bailed out over Italy's Po Valley. He and another member of the crew were rescued by partisans and sheltered for several months until the end of the war.

Chappuis, who had been a backup tailback on Michigan's 1942 team, wasn't certain he wanted to play any more football when he returned to the university in 1946. Returning war veterans had swelled the list of varsity candidates to 125, and he wasn't certain there would be a place for him on the team. He decided to go out anyway.

"Athletes were hurrying back to college campuses, a little older, more dedicated to their ideals, and vitally concerned with education," Crisler said of the older players who had fought in World War II. "They did not want to waste time."

Though the offense of the 1947 team got all the publicity, Chappuis maintains that the defense was every bit as good. The

Bob Chappuis, the star of the 1947 Michigan football team (Ann Arbor News)

members of that unit were magicians in their own right, he said. Michigan's opponents were limited to a total of fifty-four points for the season. Only two teams scored more than a touchdown against the Wolverines.

Crisler also was a great defensive mind. For instance, he had scouted Southern Cal so thoroughly before the Rose Bowl and was such a stickler for detail that the Wolverines claimed they knew as much about the USC offense as the Trojans did. Crisler had asked his former star, Tom Harmon, who then was playing professionally in California, to scout USC. Harmon saw the Trojans play six times that season. "[Crisler] wanted to know everything, even which way the seams of the ball were turned when it was snapped," Harmon recalled years later.

Tackle Alvin Wistert recalled that when the defense would get a scouting report, Crisler would go over it, telling the players, " 'Before they go across midfield, they're apt to do so and so.' Their offensive plays would unfold just as he said they would. It was amazing. I would think, 'My God, they're doing what he said they would.' "

The defense was ferocious, featuring such players as Wistert, Pete Elliott, Bob Hollway, Wally Teninga, and linebacker Dick Kempthorn. Pete Elliott later recalled that Kempthorn embodied the character of the defense: "I truly have not seen such a reckless but effective player in my life. My biggest fear on a sweep was not the opponent, but Dick. He would hurt you more coming from the inside to help with the tackle than any opponent. He hit everyone near the ball-carrier, and extremely hard. I went to great lengths to convince him that I was a sure tackler."

Michigan opened the season with a 55–0 win over Michigan State and its new coach, Clarence "Biggie" Munn, a former Crisler assistant. Kempthorn, who would become better known for his defensive efforts, scored a touchdown in his first varsity game. He had a brief conversation later in the locker room with assistant coach Bennie Oosterbaan, who told him, "Big boy, they all won't come that easy. You haven't been hit yet." Kempthorn agreed.

The next three did come easy. The Wolverines scored four touchdowns in the first nine minutes, including one on a 60-yard pass from Chappuis to Bob Mann, and rolled to a 49–13 win against Stanford the following weekend. A week later,

Chappuis and Mann hooked up again, this time for 70 yards, and Michigan rolled again, this time 69–0 against Pittsburgh. The impressive Pitt win moved the Wolverines into first place ahead of Notre Dame in the Associated Press poll, because the Irish had beaten the same Pitt team by only thirty-four points.

Following a 49–21 win at Northwestern, Hilkene sensed that the team was becoming somewhat overconfident, and he worried that such an attitude could be disastrous with tough Minnesota next up on the schedule. The Michigan captain convened a players' meeting at the Union. The meeting was serious, almost grim. Many players spoke. The players agreed that they were taking too much for granted, and they resolved to prove themselves all over again against the Gophers.

Before adjourning the meeting, Hilkene said: "If anyone has any personal gripes, now is the time to let it be known." The subsequent hushed silence was interrupted by a single hand raised in the second row. Rifenburg, who had a knack for easing tension with laughter, stood up and said with a straight face: "Bruce, I have a complaint. Frankly, I have not been getting enough publicity lately."

While his teammates laughed hysterically, Rifenburg elaborated. He complained that a reporter from *Time* magazine had been in town all week, interviewing Chappuis for a cover story, and hadn't contacted him for his prewritten, condensed biography. Rifenburg's timing could not have been better.

Crisler had started to sense an overconfidence on the part of his players the week before the Northwestern game. Hilkene recalled that the team was surprised to discover that Crisler was in an indignant mood during the pregame meeting. The coach implied that the Northwestern ground crew had deliberately used dull blades in lawn mowers, leaving the grass on the playing field a little longer than usual. High grass supposedly slowed fast running backs. Crisler even had his players believing that he sus-pected the watering hose had been left on too long, which also would have made it difficult for Michigan's backs to cut or run. Not long after the game, Hilkene recalled, it occurred to Michigan players that the field had been in excellent condition.

The homecoming game against Minnesota was a battle, as Hilkene had expected. The Gophers didn't have much in the way of offense, but their defense was the biggest the Wolverines faced all season and was intimidating. When Minnesota scored an early touchdown to take a 6–0 lead, it was the first time the Wolverines had trailed all season. Worse, Michigan's offense had completely stalled: With less than a minute remaining in the first half, the Wolverines had been held to minus 5 total yards.

With the ball at Minnesota's 40 yard line, Yerges called a time-out to remind his teammates that they had not trailed at halftime all season. He then called for the longest pass in Michigan's playbook, Chappuis to Bump Elliott. Chappuis, who'd been bothered all afternoon by Minnesota's rush, wor-ried that he would not have enough time to make a deep throw. He asked Elliott: "If I don't have much time to look for you, do you have any idea where you might be?" Elliott replied: "Just throw it toward the corner, and I'll see if I can get there."

As Chappuis faded back and looked downfield, he recog-nized that Minnesota's Leo Nomellini and Clayton Tonne-maker were both bearing down on him. He immediately heaved the ball toward the right corner of the end zone. As Chappuis lay on the ground, he heard the roar of the Michigan Stadium crowd. He knew Elliott had "gotten there." The 40-yard touchdown play and Jim Brieske's extra point gave Michigan a 7–6 halftime lead. Gene Derricotte's 21-yard touchdown run gave the Wolverines a 13–6 win, but the close margin prompted voters to drop Michigan to number two in the AP poll behind Notre Dame.

With a decisive road game at Illinois next, Crisler tweaked his special teams. Michigan had returned punts to the wide side of the field all season. Against the Fighting Illini, the Wolverines set up their blocking to the short side of the field. The new strategy paid immediate and important dividends. Bump Elliott fielded a Dike Eddleman punt at his own 26 yard line, started to his left toward the wide side of the field, and then reversed field and headed up the right sideline 74 yards for a touchdown. Illinois eventually tied the game, but a 52-yard Chappuis-to-Elliott pass set up a touchdown run by Hank Fonde that gave the Wolverines a 14–7 win.

Ann Arbor began to buzz with Rose Bowl speculation, which concerned Crisler. He forbade his players to utter the words *Rose Bowl*. But, after the Wolverines ran their record to 7–0 with a 35–0 win against Indiana, Michigan ticket manager Don Weir was forced to acknowledge that a trip to Pasadena was possible. Thousands of fans already were requesting Rose Bowl tickets. Weir sent out a letter informing them that no tickets were available yet and that an announcement about tickets would be made later.

"The Rose Bowl was something we talked about in team meetings in terms of what could be accomplished," Weisenburger recalled in a 1997 interview with the *Ann Arbor News*. "If you got to go once in a career, it was the thrill of a lifetime. But we didn't talk about it all the time. We knew that if we did our job, that would be the end result."

A win at Wisconsin in the season's next-to-last game would give the Wolverines the Big Nine championship, but weather conditions in Madison that weekend were miserable. Overnight rain, sleet, and snow had turned the Camp Randall

Stadium field to mud. Sleet fell during the game. A worried Crisler decided to play it safe and wait for the breaks to come Michigan's way. He told his quarterback, Yerges, not to take any chances. Yerges had other ideas. For the first time any player could remember, Crisler's instructions were ignored.

Leading 7–0, Michigan was faced with a fourth and one at the Badgers' 4 yard line. As the Wolverines huddled, they expected a call to Weisenburger up the middle or a quick handoff to Elliott. Instead, Yerges called a pass play. The players were stunned. All of them were convinced Yerges had been knocked senseless on the previous play. But the Wolverines were disciplined, and one of Crisler's rules was that when the quarterback stepped into the huddle, no one else was allowed to say anything. Chappuis threw a touchdown pass, to Yerges, and the Wolverines rolled to a 40–6 win that clinched the championship and a trip to the Rose Bowl.

After the Wolverines scored their fortieth point, Rifenburg looked at his teammates in the huddle and offered that perhaps it was now safe to mention the reward they'd just earned, and he spelled out R-O-S-E-B-O-W-L. The players all burst out laughing. Rifenburg recalled later that he was certain the capacity Wisconsin crowd was now convinced the Wolverines had cracked under the pressure of the championship chase.

That left only the Ohio State game. The Buckeyes won just twice that season, but Coach Wes Fesler promised a pep rally crowd the night before the game that his team would stun the Wolverines, who once again were number one in the AP poll. Though a heavy underdog, Ohio State put up a fight before Michigan prevailed, 21–0.

The final AP poll was then taken at the end of the regular season, and the national champion was determined at that point. After Notre Dame trounced Southern Cal, 38–7, in Los

Bump Elliott (left) and his brother Pete were two-way standouts for Michigan's Big Nine championship team in 1947. They later became Big Ten coaching rivals in the 1960s, Bump at Michigan and Pete at Illinois.

(Bentley Historical Library)

Angeles in the season finale, the voters awarded the title to Notre Dame, giving the Irish 107 first-place votes to Michigan's 25. But the debate was far from over, because the Wolverines still had a bowl game to play—against that same Southern Cal team.

Chappuis and Bump Elliott were named All-Americans after the season. Chappuis, who led the conference in total offense for the second consecutive season, was runner-up to Notre Dame's Johnny Lujack in the Heisman Trophy voting. Michigan led the nation in total offense, averaging 412.7 yards a game. The Wolverines also had the best passing average, 173.9 yards. Elliott, the only two-way player on the team, led the league in scoring with fifty-four points, and he was voted Michigan's and the Big Nine's most valuable player.

Grantland Rice, the dean of the nation's sportswriters, scoffed at the idea of Southern Cal upsetting Michigan. He wrote: "There are 10 teams in the country that could beat the Trojans in this Rose Bowl game, and one of those teams is

Michigan." USC coach Jeff Cravath stated publicly after the regular season that "this year's Trojan team is one of the poorest we have had in the last decade. . . . Don't get me wrong. We will be playing the full sixty minutes against Michigan and might get the breaks."

Such talk concerned Crisler, who again worried about the possibility of his players becoming overconfident. He told them before they left for the Rose Bowl: "You are going out to California to play a football game. Southern Cal is a good team, so don't underrate it. You will be praised and told how good you are. I only hope you men will properly evaluate this praise and not let it go to your head. Flattery is lethal."

Michigan left Ann Arbor December 18 on the Mercury bound for Chicago. There, they boarded the Santa Fe Super Chief for the trip to California. Special cars were assigned to Michigan's traveling party of 104, which included forty-four players. Santa Fe company officials added a final touch for the trip, arranging to have a piano in the club car after learning that Dan Dworsky was an accomplished pianist. The trip west took three nights. Players, who were used to train travel, passed the time by playing cards or by singing along with Dworsky.

When the team arrived in California, Hilkene told reporters: "We are not here for a joy ride." But there were plenty of distractions. Chrysler Corporation provided chauffeur-driven DeSotos that were painted maize and blue. The Wolverines attended a rehearsal for Bob Hope's radio program. They toured several movie studios, including Paramount's, where they watched part of the filming of *Foreign Affairs* and *Sealed Verdict*. They met Charlie McCarthy and Edgar Bergen, Loretta Young, Marlene Dietrich, and Ray Milland.

Bump and Pete Elliott played golf with Bing Crosby. Pete Elliott, who earned four letters in golf at Michigan, shot a 44;

Bump Elliott shot a 39; and Crosby finished with a 37. Afterward, Crosby drove the players back to their hotel in his convertible. "Here we were, riding down Sunset Boulevard, and Crosby is singing to us," recalled Chappuis, who went along to watch. "People pay millions of dollars to hear him sing. We got it all for free."

According to one news story, Chappuis was warned by a Michigan fan to avoid shaking hands with comedian Joe E. Brown. The fan wrote to the athletic department: "Do you recall the World Series in Detroit when Joe E. Brown shook hands with Schoolboy Rowe and ruined him for the rest of the series? That was no accident. Keep Chappuis away from Brown and those other movie stars, or he won't throw many passes on January 1." Chappuis never met Brown during the trip, but he says he would have shaken hands with the comedian if he had. Both were Toledo natives.

Weisenburger recalled that the distractions were never a problem for the Wolverines: "We had a curfew—I think it was 11 o'clock—but there was no bed check. We were on our honesty. I'm not aware of anyone who abused it, but I'm sure there were probably one or two who did."

Crisler got a scare the week before the game, when the automobile in which he was riding caught fire en route from practice at Brookside Park to the team's headquarters, the Huntington Hotel. An Associated Press story chronicled the incident: "Displaying all the nimble speed for which his backs are feared and famed, Crisler escaped with nothing more than a case of wholesale hot foot."

The team's practice field was right next to the Rose Bowl, which is surrounded by mountains. The '47 players wondered if Crisler worried for good reason or just for show, but the coach was convinced Southern Cal had spies watching practices from homes on the hillsides. "Fritz was always concerned about spying, and he would accuse people who lived around there of doing it," Bump Elliott recalled. "He'd send managers up into the hills to run people off. I'm pretty sure it was mostly a show for us, because I think it was his imagination. But he used it to our benefit."

During one practice the team got a visit from Crisler's former coach, eighty-five-year-old Amos Alonzo Stagg. Gathered in a huddle of players, Stagg offered a victory formula for the New Year's Day game: "Score the first touchdown and then keep on scoring." After watching Michigan's intricate offensive formations for a while, Stagg told a reporter that he had never taught Crisler "all of that fancy stuff."

With a Rose Bowl crowd of 93,000 looking on, Michigan struggled early against the bigger Trojans. Ten minutes into the game, Weisenburger scored the first of his three touchdowns from a yard out, and the rout was on. The Wolverines threw for the other four touchdowns. Kempthorn's first-half interception thwarted Southern Cal's only serious scoring threat.

"What astonished me was the ease with which our line opened holes for us," Weisenburger said. "It was one of those days when everything clicked. We just had good success. But I can tell you that no one for a moment thought we would win by a score like that."

Despite a sore leg, Chappuis completed fourteen of twenty-four passes and ran for 91 yards. Weisenburger gained 95 yards on his spinners. The Wolverines produced a record 491 yards on offense. The performance so stunned columnist Braven Dyer of the *Los Angeles Times* that he wrote: "Aw, well, it wasn't as bad as we expected; it was worse." Columnist Jim Murray wrote: "Southern Cal lost the toss and grew steadily worse." Chappuis said: "I thought that was a great line."

Master Motivator

Fritz Crisler was as good a motivator as he was a strategist and an innovator, and he proved it just days before the 1948 Rose Bowl game against Southern Cal.

Halfback Bob Chappuis, who'd been runner-up in the Heisman Trophy balloting, pulled a hamstring in practice the Monday before the game. After Crisler was informed about the nature of the injury by the team's trainer, Jim Hunt, the coach responded: "Good thing it didn't happen to someone who could run." Chappuis jumped up off the ground and limped to the huddle.

"I don't believe he felt that way, but he didn't want the rest of the team to know he was worried," Chappuis recalled. "The idea was: We could get along without Chappuis. Bruce Hilkene told me many years later that Crisler's reaction made him feel a lot better. It was as if to say, even if we lose an important player, we'll win anyway. Fritz got exactly the reaction he wanted. He was a genius at that."

How did Chappuis perform in the bowl game? His leg was sore, but the pain didn't slow him. He finished with 91 yards rushing, and he passed for 139 yards and two touchdowns. He was named the game's most outstanding player.

The Wolverines handled USC so impressively that the Associated Press took the unprecedented step of conducting another poll. Sports editors nationally were asked to choose again between 10–0 Michigan and 9–0 Notre Dame. When the results of the second poll were revealed on January 6, Michigan won with 226 first-place votes to Notre Dame's 119. Both schools claim the national title from that season. Michigan players were awarded national championship rings.

The Rose Bowl was the last game ever coached by Crisler, who retired the following March after ten seasons as Michigan's head coach.

"The 1947 team was one of the best I've seen in college football," Crisler said years later. "It was a remarkable group of people who came as close to perfection on the football field as any coach could expect.

"After they graduated, it seemed like a good time to step down as head coach. There was not much that could happen afterward which would be more rewarding for a coach."

The 1947 Season

Date	Opponent	Result
September 27	vs. Michigan St.	W, 55–0
October 4	vs. Stanford	W, 49–13
October 11	vs. Pittsburgh	W, 69–0
October 18	at Northwestern	W, 49–21
October 25	vs. Minnesota	W, 13–6
November 1	at Illinois	W, 14–7
November 8	vs. Indiana	W, 35–0
November 15	at Wisconsin	W, 40–6
November 22	vs. Ohio State	W, 21–0
January 1	vs. Southern Cal	W, 49–0

Roses Bloom in the Snow

The 1950 Ohio State Game

It is a testament to the significance and tradition of rivalry between Michigan and Ohio State that the strangest game ever played in the series is known, simply, as "The Snow Bowl."

Though other college games were played under similar miserable weather conditions that Thanksgiving weekend in 1950, no other one captured the imagination of the nation enough to rate a nickname. This one did, almost certainly, because it involved the Wolverines and the Buckeyes. "We played Illinois two years in a row in the snow and cold, but the game everyone always remembers is the one against Ohio State," former Wolverine Don Peterson recalled.

There are any number of good reasons for that.

Historically, the Michigan–Ohio State game is important in terms of the Big Ten championship race. That was the case in 1950: Michigan's improbable 9–3 win, coupled with Northwestern's stunning 14–7 upset of Illinois the same day, sent the Wolverines to the Rose Bowl. The outcome prompted one newspaper to declare in a headline that roses really did bloom in the snow.

Statistically speaking, the game was an anomaly. Michigan did not get a first down, gained only 27 yards rushing, did

Only 50,503 hardy spectators, out of a paid attendance of more than 80,000, braved heavy snow, zero-degree temperatures, and 30-mile-per-hour winds to watch Michigan defeat Ohio State, 9–3, in "The Snow Bowl" game in Ohio Stadium. (Bentley Historical Library)

not complete a single one of its nine pass attempts, and tied the modern NCAA record by punting an astounding twenty-four times. Yet, the Wolverines still won.

"It wasn't a football game. It was a matter of getting the ball back and kicking it," said Carl Kreager, who, as Michigan's center, played a critical role in implementing that strategy. "I have often said this to close friends: We were in the right place at the right time. It was the kind of day that the only thing to do was kick the football. We prevailed because of that."

Unfortunately, few Michigan fans were on hand to witness the triumph. They couldn't get to Columbus. And the ones who did get there had a difficult time getting home.

The day before the game, the worst blizzard since 1913 paralyzed the Midwest and Northeast and dipped as far south as Tennessee. Record low temperatures gripped the entire eastern half of the nation. At least 9 inches of snow alone had fallen on Columbus Saturday morning. That wasn't the worst of it, because the Wolverines had played in snow the weekend before at home against Illinois. But by game time, the temperature was near zero, and the snow was swirling around Ohio Stadium, driven by northwest winds of up to 30 miles per hour. "Most people would not let kids go outside in conditions like that," ex-Wolverine Charles Ortmann said. "You and I would not go outside to get the newspaper on a day like that. But here we were, trying to play football."

Not everyone tried. The game between Pitt and Penn State in Pittsburgh was postponed. Other schools did play. In Knoxville, Tennessee, workers removed more than one hundred tons of snow from the field for the Kentucky–Tennessee game. At Athens, Georgia, only 2,000 spectators braved the wind and twelve-degree temperature to watch the Georgia–Furman game. Any game in the East or Midwest was played on a frozen field and, in many cases, with snow on the ground or falling.

A total of 82,700 tickets had been sold for the game. Amazingly, 50,503 fans made it through the turnstiles. Ohio State officials did not bother to take tickets, so any spectator hardy (or foolhardy) enough to brave the elements could walk right in. Former Michigan players aren't certain about the accuracy of the attendance figure, but they admit it was hard to see across the field, let alone to the upper reaches of the stadium known as the Horseshoe. The players did notice, however, that some groups of fans started bonfires in the stands to keep warm, most likely using game programs and paper trash as fuel.

The two athletic directors, Michigan's Fritz Crisler and Ohio State's Richard Larkins, discussed right up until the scheduled kickoff time the possibility of postponing the game. Ohio State coach Wes Fesler reportedly favored doing that, but Michigan officials were adamant about playing. That didn't surprise Michigan players, who were used to playing and practicing in lousy weather. They expected to play. Besides, the Wolverines knew Crisler's reputation for being tight with a buck: He would not have wanted to pay for a second trip to Columbus to make up the game. The athletic directors eventually reasoned that if some 50,000 fans had turned out, it would be unfair to send them home without seeing a game.

While the athletic directors debated whether or not to play, several hundred stadium workers struggled to remove the frozen, snow-covered tarpaulins that covered the field. Several area gas stations contributed four-wheel-drive vehicles to assist. The tarpaulins had been little help in protecting the field, which was icy in many spots. Snow continued to fall. By scheduled kickoff workers had to clear several more inches off the field, a process that delayed the start of the game by forty-five minutes.

Many times, the blowing snow created whiteout conditions. Michigan players had a hard time seeing the Ohio State sideline. Ortmann recalled that on several plays, he could not see from his safety position Ohio State runners lined up in their backfield. The few times it was necessary to measure for a first down, a stadium worker with a shovel would accompany the chain gang to clear the field so that the proper yard line was found.

Until the blizzard blew in on Friday, the discussion around the Big Nine—Michigan State was not yet a member—centered on what shaped up to be one of the most intriguing races in conference history. Ohio State, which at one point had been ranked number one in the nation, could not go to the Rose Bowl because of the conference's no-repeat rule. The Buckeyes were one of four teams that had a shot at the championship on the season's final weekend. There were any number of combinations of wins, losses, and ties that would have sent either Michigan, Wisconsin, or Illinois to Pasadena for New Year's Day.

By program standards Michigan was having a tough season. The Wolverines entered the game with a 4–3–1 overall record, having lost to Michigan State, Army, and Illinois and tied Minnesota. Following a 7–0 loss at home to Illinois on November 4, Michigan was 2–3–1 and had been outscored 75–73. But the Wolverines regrouped by beating Indiana and Northwestern, setting the stage for the climactic season finale. To get to the Rose Bowl, they had to beat the 6–2 Buckeyes, and they needed some help: Northwestern had to upset Illinois in Evanston. "The feeling on the team was that we would beat Ohio State," former Wolverine Leo Koceski said. "The trouble was, we needed Northwestern to win, too, and no one expected that to happen."

The Wolverines made what at the time was their usual road trip to Columbus. They traveled Friday by bus to Toledo, where they stayed the night at the Commodore Perry Hotel. Early Saturday morning, they boarded a train bound for Columbus. It was snowing, but the players weren't concerned because they'd played in snow and just-below-freezing temperatures before. "No one thought much about [the weather]," Peterson said. "Certainly, no one thought it would be as bad as it was."

The train trip south ended on a siding a short distance from Ohio Stadium. As they waited on the warm train cars for the short walk to the locker room, many of the players stared through the windows at the arctic conditions outside and at fans struggling to get to the stadium. Some fans crossed the railroad tracks right next to the train and tried to make their way down a small embankment. Most would hit a slick patch of ice and fall on their backsides. "It got to be a little funny thing, and the whole team sat and watched," Ortmann recalled. Rather than taking on a serious attitude for the big game, the Wolverines were laughing heartily at the spectacle outside. By game time the players were totally relaxed. Michigan coaches weren't amused, however. Peterson recalled that when assistant George Ceithamel entered the car and saw what was going on, he angrily demanded to know what the players thought they were doing.

Michigan equipment manager Henry Hatch had packed long winter underwear, but the players still grabbed for anything extra they could wear under their uniforms. Surprisingly, only one pair of gloves was available: a fine leather dress set that belonged to assistant coach Dick Kempthorn. He offered up the gloves for the cause. The logical person to wear them was Kreager, but the center refused because he worried they would hamper his ability to make the many snaps required in Michigan's single-wing offense. Ortmann, the halfback and punter who took nearly all of Kreager's snaps when the Wolverines were on offense, was the next obvious choice, but he also refused—at least he did for a while. Ortmann also played on defense, so he never left the field. Before long, he realized that having frozen hands would be worse than having gloves on them. As offensive players headed to the sideline near the end of the first quarter, Ortmann instructed Kreager to bring the gloves back with him the next time the offense came back on the field. Ortmann wore the gloves the rest of the game.

Ortmann had a busy afternoon. He'd been the team's punter at the start of the season, but he'd been forced to stop after injuring his ankle in the season opener against Michigan State. After that, he'd only punted in practice. Tony Momsen had punted for the next seven games. Inexplicably, Momsen asked Ortmann if he would punt against Ohio State. Ortmann did—a school-record twenty-four times! Ohio State punted twenty-one times—the most ever for a Michigan opponent. The combined forty-five punts is still an NCAA single-game record.

Though Ortmann gets much credit for his punting exploits, he and other teammates insist that the real hero of the victory was Kreager, who did not make a bad snap all afternoon. "I could have shut my eyes and the ball would have hit my hands," Ortmann said about his center. "The ball never missed where my hands were. He was a heck of a football player. He knows how I feel about him." Kreager believes his contribution tends to be exaggerated because Ohio State's center played so poorly in the game. "[Ohio State's Vic] Janowicz played shortstop back there," Kreager recalled. "We blocked two of their punts because the ball was not getting back to the punter. That made it look like it was more difficult. I got a lot of help in the huddle. The other guys would let me put my hands under their armpits to keep them warm. I couldn't wear gloves and center the ball, particularly on punts. It was a real team effort. I was lucky the guys helped me out."

Ohio State was able to complete three of its eighteen pass attempts for 25 yards and rushed for another 16 yards, but any real movement on offense by either team was almost always the result of a broken play. "We'd bust loose for 3 or 4 yards and then hit a patch of ice and slip down," Ortmann said. "It quickly became a defensive game."

That Michigan made no first downs was as much due to Coach Bennie Oosterbaan's strategy as to the effectiveness of the Ohio State defense. Rather than risk a block by waiting until fourth down to punt, the Wolverines would punt on third down and sometimes even earlier. It was not an unusual strategy, at least not in Michigan football history: Fielding H. Yost was notorious for punting early in a series in an attempt to gain the advantage in field position. "We went in with the thought in mind that if we didn't make [a first down] on third down, field position would become very important," Peterson said. "We played it strategically."

It was not surprising, then, that in a game with almost no offense and a record number of punts that the game would ultimately turn on three blocked punts: two by the Wolverines and one by the Buckeyes.

Early in the game, Ohio State's Janowicz boomed a punt that rolled dead at Michigan's 6 yard line. The Wolverines failed to move the ball and attempted to punt from there, but Joe Campanella blocked it and the Buckeyes recovered at the Michigan 8.

Janowicz attempted to pass on first down, but the Wolverines chased him back to his 29 yard line. He threw the ball away but was penalized for intentional grounding. The Buckeyes wound up with the ball on their 34. They got 13 yards of the loss back on one pass play, but that was it. From 27 yards away, Janowicz slammed a field-goal attempt into the blowing snow and through the uprights. On this day those three points gave Ohio State what appeared to be an insurmountable lead. As play continued, neither team appeared to want the ball and elected to punt on any down but fourth.

After Ortmann was able to knock one of his punts out of bounds at the Ohio State 4 yard line, Janowicz attempted to punt on first down. The snap was low, and Michigan tackle Al Wahl broke through to block the kick. The ball shot out of the end zone for a safety. With 4:54 remaining in the first quarter, Ohio State clung to a 3–2 lead.

Ortmann's punting kept the Buckeyes pinned deep in their own end of the field. For the remainder of the first half, Ohio State started drives at its own 14, 10, 16, 15, 9, 14, 20, and 9 yard lines. Michigan needed some kind of break, and it got one with forty-seven seconds remaining.

Facing third and 6 at their 13 yard line, the Buckeyes elected to punt early once more. Again, the snap to Janowicz was low, and Michigan's Tony Momsen blocked the punt and fell on the ball in the end zone for a touchdown. Harry Allis kicked the extra point. It was the eighth time in series history, including the earlier safety, that a blocked punt had resulted in a score. That Momsen delivered the decisive play was appropriate: He was an Ohio native—from Toledo—and his brother, Bob, played for the Buckeyes.

Ohio State got a break on Michigan's first possession of the second half when Richard Anderson recovered a fumble at the Wolverines' 30 yard line. But on third down Michigan's Oswald Clark intercepted a Janowicz pass and the threat passed. From that point on there were punts, punts, and more punts. And more snow. By the end of the third quarter, reporters in the upper-deck press box could no longer see the players on the field.

Michigan looked to add to its lead in the fourth quarter when Allis attempted a 25-yard field goal. The kick was long enough, but it sailed wide of one of the uprights. Allis, an end who played on offense and defense, was Michigan's main kicker for three seasons. He led the Big Ten in scoring in 1948. Ironically, that miss in Columbus was the only field goal he attempted in his career.

Because of the delay at the start of the game, the Illinois–Northwestern game finished before the Michigan–Ohio State game did. Late in the fourth quarter, Koceski returned to the huddle and informed his teammates that Northwestern had pulled the upset the Wolverines needed. Seconds later, the Northwestern–Illinois score was announced over the public-address system at Ohio Stadium. All the Wolverines had to do was hang on, and they would be headed to the Rose Bowl.

There was one more scare left for the Wolverines, however. In attempting to clear the snow before the start of the game, stadium workers pushed what they could back to the perimeter of the field. They left a 4- to 5-inch buildup of snow in both end zones. Janowicz's final punt of the game rolled into the end zone, but when the ball hit the snow buildup, it came to a stop and rolled back onto the playing field. Ortmann insisted that the ball had rolled into the end zone, but officials ruled that the ball was down inside the Michigan 1. Barely a minute remained in the game.

"We decided to punt on first down," Ortmann recalled. "We shifted into the single wing, and then quickly went to punt formation. My mind was wandering at that point. I kept seeing the headlines: 'Punt blocked! Michigan loses!' Fortunately, I got the punt away, and we ended up winning."

Michigan finished 4–1–1 for a .750 winning percentage. Ohio State and Wisconsin tied for second at .714. There was one small consolation for the Buckeyes: Janowicz would go on to win the Heisman Trophy.

As Michigan players celebrated in their locker room, Oosterbaan told reporters: "Imagine having a great team like Fesler had and not being able to use it because of the conditions. Naturally, I'm happy to have won, but the conditions were such that it wasn't a fair test of football." Fesler, who had coached his last game for the Buckeyes, agreed: "You can't take a thing away from Michigan. We both faced the same conditions. I certainly agree with Bennie, however, that it was not a test of gridiron skill."

With the season over Michigan players were free to return to their homes for what was left of the Thanksgiving holiday weekend. A number of players chose to remain in Columbus rather than battle the elements, and they were stranded for several days. Koceski's family had driven to the game from Pittsburgh. It took them four days to get home.

The reward for the Wolverines was a trip to someplace a whole lot warmer—sunny Pasadena—but they were not favored to beat Cal, a 9–0–1 team that was ranked fourth nationally. The Golden Bears were making their third consecutive trip to the Rose Bowl, and this time they were expected to end the Pacific Conference's four-game losing streak to the Big Nine. "We got a lot of bad press out there, and it motivated us," Kreager recalled. "Maybe we weren't the best team in the conference, but we were the champions."

The first and second halves were like completely different games. Cal dominated the first half, getting ten first downs to Michigan's two. The Wolverines gained fifteen first downs in the second half to the Golden Bears' two. Cal had a 192–65 advantage

Fullback Don Dufek (in letter jacket) holds the trophy he earned as the outstanding player in the 1951 Rose Bowl. Dufek scored both Michigan touchdowns in a 14–6 win against California. (Bentley Historical Library)

in total yards in the first half. Michigan had a 226–52 advantage in total yards in the second half.

Cal led 6–0 at halftime, thanks to Jim Marinos's 39-yard touchdown pass to Bob Cummings. The extra-point attempt failed. The lead could have been bigger, but Pete Schabarum's 73-yard end run for an apparent touchdown was nullified by a holding penalty.

Michigan was held scoreless until the fourth quarter, when fullback Don Dufek ran four identical plays starting from the Cal 4 yard line. He finally scored on fourth and 1,

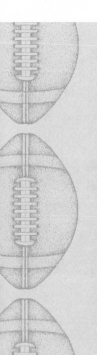

Back from the Blizzard

Unlike many teammates and Michigan fans who were stuck in Columbus and central Ohio for several days following "The Snow Bowl," halfback Charles Ortmann caught the last train out of Columbus that afternoon and then was able to get a bus from Toledo to Ann Arbor. By 9:30 that night, he stopped by the City Club to visit the owners, Ruth and George Earle.

"No one could believe I was back from the game," Ortmann said. "Here's the highlight of the story. . . . I came back [two or three] years later after graduation, and the owner was waiting to tell me what he said was the funniest story in the world. They were open for lunch that Tuesday [after the game], and the door slams open. A fellow walked in smelling of alcohol, and he announced that he was the first guy to make it back from Columbus. They told him he wasn't. Nobody could believe that a guy in the game got back the same day."

and Allis's extra point put the Wolverines ahead to stay. Dufek would score again later in the quarter, this time from 7 yards out. Allis's second PAT capped the scoring. Michigan went home with a 14–6 win. Dufek was named the game's most valuable player.

As players do today when they play in a bowl game, the Michigan players received several gifts for their participation in the Rose Bowl. The most memorable of the presents? Each Wolverine received a pair of leather dress gloves, identical to the ones Ortmann had worn in "The Snow Bowl."

"The Snow Bowl" at a Glance

Category	Michigan	Ohio State
Plays	7	70
First downs	0	3
Rushing yards	27	16
Passing yards	0	25
Total yards	27	41
Passing	0 for 9	3 for 18
Turnovers	1	3
Punts*	24	21
Penalty yards	25	30

* The two teams combined to punt the ball for almost 1,400 yards.

The Big Three

Michigan's Heisman Trophy Winners

The numbers appear to be incongruous: Michigan, the Division I program with the most wins in college football history, has produced just three Heisman Trophy winners.

And, yet, understanding that the focus at Michigan has always been on the team rather than any one individual, the numbers are understandable. Although many schools have resorted to Madison Avenue advertising campaigns to promote their Heisman candidates, Michigan has prided itself on never having done so.

"That's just the way it is at Michigan," said former All-American halfback Bob Chappuis, who finished second to Notre Dame's Johnny Lujack in the 1947 Heisman balloting. "We just didn't promote the individual at Michigan, and that is the way it should be. I played for Fritz Crisler, and he believed in a team effort. Bo Schembechler and Gary Moeller were the same way, and so is Lloyd Carr."

Michigan's three Heisman Trophy winners—Tom Harmon in 1940, Desmond Howard in 1991, and Charles Woodson in 1997—all succeeded in that fashion. Harmon was, without question, the premier player of his day. Howard had an offensive season unlike any other in Big Ten history. Woodson's versatility and flair for making big plays in the biggest games helped him to become the first primarily defensive player to win the award.

The Wolverines have always insisted that any individual award be achieved out of the success of the entire team. As Coach Lloyd Carr once said: "If the team is successful, there are enough accolades to go around for everyone."

Harmon, Howard, and Woodson received the ultimate accolade: the Heisman.

"Old 98": Tom Harmon

While Fritz Crisler was completing his final season as head coach at Princeton in the fall of 1937, freshman Tom Harmon was still learning his way around the campus. But if Harmon wasn't yet a familiar figure to his fellow students, he was causing a stir at Ferry Field, where the Michigan football team practiced.

A marvelous high school athlete in Gary, Indiana, who'd earned fourteen letters in track, baseball, basketball, and football, Harmon was already demonstrating that he might be the player who could return the Michigan football program, which had slipped in the latter years of Coach Harry Kipke's tenure, to its place among the nation's elite. Kipke twice called the freshman team to engage the varsity in a gamelike scrimmage. The freshmen won twice, 7–6 and 21–0, though the games were extended in the hope the varsity could gain the upper hand.

If ever a coach and player complemented each other, it was Crisler and Harmon. Harmon possessed myriad football talents—speed, power, fearlessness, and a great sense of anticipation—and Crisler was an inventive genius who was always looking for ways to improve and refine his single-wing offense. In Harmon the new Michigan coach had the triple-threat running back who could be utilized to his fullest as a runner, passer, and punter.

Tom Harmon during the final minutes of Michigan's 7–6 loss at Minnesota in 1940. The loss cost Michigan a chance to win the Big Nine championship that season.
(Bentley Historical Library)

To Fritz—
In sincere appreciation for all you have done—My best wishes always to not only the greatest coach in the world but also the greatest guy—Ole "98" will take you as the All American coach every day—
Sincerely
Tom—

"I am so thankful for the circumstances that placed me under Fritz Crisler, the man I believe to be the greatest football coach the game has ever seen," Harmon told the *Ann Arbor News* in 1968. "I am certain that were it not for Fritz, this halfback would never have gained the honors that came my way during my three seasons at Michigan."

The elusive Harmon did benefit from one of Crisler's innovations: the tear-away jersey. Often, the best a tackler could do was to grab a handful of Harmon's jersey. A tackler once ripped Harmon's numerals "98" off the jersey, and then he later asked the Michigan star to autograph them for him. Michigan officials estimated that Harmon went through a dozen or more jerseys a season, and he sometimes changed them as often as three times a game. Crisler's favorite photograph of Harmon was one taken in the final minutes of Michigan's 7–6 loss at Minnesota in 1940. Harmon is standing in the rain, spattered with mud from head to foot. His sleeve is ripped off, and a large section of his shirt is torn out.

Harmon wasn't the only outstanding player on the Crisler's first three Michigan teams, but he came to symbolize the Wolverines' return to prominence. His backfield mates included the bruising Forest Evashevski and Bob Westfall, arguably the greatest fullback in school history. The line of Ed Frutig, Al Wistert, Ralph Fritz, Milo Sukup, and Bob Kolesar was formidable.

That the Wolverines did not achieve more notoriety or win a championship as a team was due to one failure: They could not defeat Minnesota. Three of the four losses Michigan suffered during Harmon's college career were to the Golden Gophers, in part because he was held scoreless in those games. Harmon insisted until his death in 1990 that the 1940 Michigan team, which finished 7–1, was the finest ever to play for Michigan, and he always blamed himself for the team's failure against Minnesota. During that 7–6 loss to Minnesota in 1940, Harmon missed a critical extra point and slipped in the mud at the Gophers' 1 yard line to end another scoring threat.

"Tom Harmon was probably the greatest football player Michigan has ever had," former Michigan sports information director Will Perry said in 1990, on learning of Harmon's death. "He was truly a legendary sports hero. At a time in this country when there was no television, everyone knew who Tom Harmon was. He might have been the greatest all-around player in the history of college football."

Tom Harmon runs against Michigan State during the 1940 season. Michigan won the game, 21–14. Note the wing and the small "S" on the Michigan State helmets. (Bentley Historical Library)

The Toughest Battles

Tom Harmon survived his battles on the college gridiron in good shape, but he was not nearly as fortunate in two close brushes with death as a pilot in World War II.

Harmon was reported missing in April 1943, when a plane he was piloting crashed in the jungles of Dutch Guiana. He was able to make his way after six days to an air base in the South American country. No other members of the crew survived.

Eight months later, the P-38 Lightning in which Harmon was flying was shot down by Japanese Zeros over China. Harmon shot down two Zeros before being hit. He suffered second-degree burns on both legs and also suffered burns to his face after the cockpit in which he was riding burst into flames. Harmon lived for thirty-two days behind enemy lines with the aid of Chinese guerillas. For his military heroics he was awarded the Silver Star and the Purple Heart.

Harmon played for the Los Angeles Rams from 1946–47, but his legs had been debilitated by the injuries and he was unable to match the football success he'd enjoyed in college.

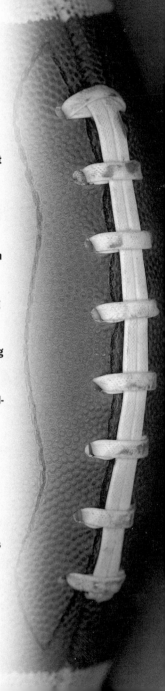

In his three seasons at Michigan, Harmon gained 2,134 yards rushing on 398 carries, completed 101 of 233 passes for 1,396 yards, scored 33 touchdowns, and led the nation in scoring in 1939 and 1940. Harmon set the school record for total offense in twenty-four games; quarterback Rick Leach needed forty-four games in the mid-1970s to eclipse it. A two-time All-American, Harmon won the Maxwell Trophy as the Big Nine's most valuable player in 1940. His number, 98, was retired after his graduation.

Every game in which Harmon participated was filled with sparkling moments, but many Michigan fans of that era believed he turned in his three best performances on the road.

In the next-to-last game of the 1939 season, Harmon delivered possibly the greatest run in school history to help the Wolverines pull out a 19–17 win against Penn at Philadelphia's Franklin Field. Harmon's run covered 63 yards and consumed more than thirty seconds. He twice reversed his field and retreated as far back as Michigan's 21 yard line before finally dashing through a host of would-be tacklers for the go-ahead touchdown.

In the 1940 season opener against California at Berkeley, Harmon scored on runs of 95, 85, 64, and 23 yards as Michigan won handily, 41–0. The Michigan star so frustrated the Cal players that a spectator jumped out of the stands and attempted to tackle Harmon. He had no better luck than the Golden Bears did.

Harmon would save his very best for last. Before 73,648 rain-drenched spectators at Ohio Stadium, he was a one-man wrecking crew during a 40–0 win against Ohio State. Harmon scored three touchdowns, passed for two more, and kicked four conversions. He carried twenty-five times and gained 139 yards. He completed eleven of his twenty-two passes for 151 yards. His three punts averaged 50 yards. He returned three punts for 81 yards. He accounted for 371 all-purpose yards. He played fifty-nine minutes of the game. When Harmon left the field after his third touchdown of the afternoon, the Ohio Stadium crowd gave him a standing ovation.

Harmon served in the Air Force in World War II and was discharged as a captain. He became sports director at KFI television in Los Angeles in 1947, and two years later, he moved to the Columbia Pacific Radio Network. He moved in 1962 to ABC radio, and his nightly sports show was syndicated to more than 400 stations nationwide. He married movie actress Elyse Knox in 1944, and the couple had three children, including son Mark, who played quarterback at UCLA and went on to become an actor.

Harmon never forgot his alma mater, and he was forever grateful for the experience he'd had there. During his last visit to Ann Arbor in 1988, Harmon told a reporter: "I am sure hundreds of football players have enjoyed the experience of wearing the maize and blue, but none has enjoyed it more, or appreciated it more, than this very lucky Irishman."

The "Magic" Man: Desmond Howard

It had been fifty-one years since Harmon had won Michigan's only Heisman Trophy. Since 1940, sixty-four All-Americans had come through Ann Arbor and Michigan teams had won twenty-one Big Ten championships and finished among the nation's top ten teams twenty-nine times. But the Heismans went elsewhere.

Except in 1991, when Desmond Howard, a wisp of a player at 5'7" and 176 pounds, grabbed the attention of college football fans everywhere with his infectious smile and his electrifying runs and acrobatic catches. He was, appropriately

Michigan's Desmond Howard races to run under a pass during his Heisman Trophy–winning season in 1991. (Bentley Historical Library)

enough, called "Magic," though the moniker irked many at rival Michigan State, who believed the nickname rightfully belonged only to former Spartans basketball star, Earvin Johnson. Coincidentally, Howard earned his nickname in the seventh grade playing basketball, after he scored twenty of his team's twenty-five points in an overtime win at a Cleveland recreation center.

Howard became the first receiver in Big Ten history to lead the conference in scoring with ninety points, and he set or tied five NCAA records and twelve single-season school records. He won both the Maxwell and Walter Camp Awards.

He was the Big Ten's Athlete of the Year, and he was named college football's offensive player by both the Associated Press and United Press International. "I've never seen anyone have a better season," then-Michigan head coach Gary Moeller said. "You can refer back to different guys who played here or elsewhere, but when you notice him in each and every game, that is something special. When he gets the ball, everyone in the stadium gets excited because you never know what he's going to do."

Though he had not been mentioned as a Heisman contender when the season began, no one was surprised four months later when he easily won the trophy. The only suspense heading into the ceremony at the Downtown Athletic Club in New York City was whether he would set a record in doing so. His 640 first-place votes, representing 85 percent of the ballots cast, were the most ever for a Heisman winner. The point differential between Howard and the runner-up, Florida State quarterback Casey Weldon, was the second-largest in the history of the award, topped only by O. J. Simpson's win over Purdue's Leroy Keyes in 1968.

Beginning with a 93-yard kickoff return and four-touchdown performance in the season opener at Boston College that kickstarted the Wolverines' 10–1 run to the Big Ten championship and the Rose Bowl, Howard's Heisman season was a montage of magnificent moments. He jumped into the national spotlight a week later with two more touchdowns, including one on a dramatic, diving catch in the fourth quarter that sealed the Wolverines' 24–14 win over Notre Dame. "The Notre Dame game was like the New Hampshire [presidential] primary," ESPN commentator Beano Cook said at the conclusion of the '91 season. "Howard took the [Heisman] lead in that game and never gave it up."

The Magic Number

Desmond Howard was not the last Michigan player to wear number 21, but he made the number a collector's item.

On walking into a local sporting goods store during his Heisman season, Howard noticed a rack full of Michigan jerseys with his number and several customers purchasing them.

"Two years ago, I went into one of those stores and never saw a number 21 jersey," Howard said in a 1991 interview with the *Ann Arbor News*. "I told people that before I leave here, they are going to be selling number 21 jerseys. I am glad to see they are selling like hotcakes."

Running back Tshimanga Biakabutuka wore number 21 for three seasons (1993–95). The Michigan athletic department retired Howard's jersey number during the 1998 season.

Though they'd seen Howard work his magic many times in practice, Michigan teammates still were stunned by the catch against the Fighting Irish. Center Matt Elliott recalled the moment: "I blocked the noseguard and put him on the ground. Then I looked up . . . and it was a long ball to Desmond. I thought, 'Hmm, I don't know if this one's gonna get there. Or if Desmond's gonna get there.' Then he accelerated at top speed, don't ask me how. He was motoring and then he accelerated even more, and then he hauled it in. Lord only knows how."

It quickly became apparent that Howard was the only candidate for the award. Although Howard was consistent—he scored at least two touchdowns in nine of Michigan's eleven regular-season games—preseason favorites Ty Detmer of Brigham Young and David Klingler of Houston, both quarterbacks, faltered early. Weldon emerged as Howard's chief challenger, but his chances were ruined when the Seminoles lost their final two games to in-state rivals Miami and Florida. The other Heisman finalist was standout Washington defensive tackle Steve Emtman, but it would take another six years before a defensive player would finally win the award.

As Harmon had done in the final game of his senior season, Howard punctuated his Heisman run with an exclamation point against Ohio State, return-ing a punt 93 yards for a touchdown. It was the sec-ond-longest scoring play in the Michigan–Ohio State series, eclipsed only by a 113-yard return of a missed field goal by Michigan's Alfred Barlow in the 1905 game. As he stepped into the end zone after his long return,

Desmond Howard races into the end zone for the first of his two touchdowns in a 24–14 win against Notre Dame.
(Bentley Historical Library)

Howard struck a familiar pose—the one on the Heisman Trophy. In less than a month, the trophy would be his.

"I never put any pressure on myself to win this award or any award," Howard said the night he accepted the Heisman. "I just wanted to play consistently week in and week out and help our team win. The only reason I couldn't completely block the Heisman out of my mind was because reporters kept asking me about it."

As he was about to leave the podium that night, Howard was asked about his mother's reaction to his receiving the award. He had seen her, live via a television hookup from Cleveland, burst into tears when his name was announced. "I think besides May 15, 1970, this will be the most memorable day of her life," Howard told reporters. Asked what happened on that date, he replied: "I was born."

A Heisman First: Charles Woodson

For a player whose game spoke volumes, Charles Woodson was a remarkably quiet guy.

That's evident in a story Fremont (Ohio) Ross High School assistant football coach Chuck Lindsey liked to tell about Woodson: "Some Tiffin kids were at the mall talking to some Fremont kids, and they were talking about Woodson. The Tiffin kids were asking if he really was that good. This went on for about fifteen minutes before one of the Fremont kids finally said, 'Why don't you ask him?' Charles had been standing right there the whole time."

Woodson's teammates on the 1997 Michigan football team, which brought home the program's first national championship in five decades, would have appreciated the anecdote because they recognized his separate personalities. There was Woodson the football player: poised, confident, and brash.

Charles Woodson slips past an Ohio State defender during his 78-yard punt return for a touchdown in the 1997 game. (Ann Arbor News)

Then, there was Woodson the college student, jealously guarding his privacy and his time with close friends.

Woodson never went looking for the spotlight, but, because of his brilliance on the field in 1997, it continually found him. He was, without question, the best player on the nation's number one defense. He had seven interceptions that season—tops in the Big Ten and second in the nation. But he was also an offensive and special teams threat. He averaged 21 yards on eleven pass receptions, 8.6 yards on thirty-three punt returns, and 5 yards on three runs. He also completed a pass and scored four touchdowns. His versatility ultimately is what put him over the top in the minds of many Heisman voters, who ignored precedence and made Woodson the first predominantly defensive player to win the award.

The Heisman finalists that season were a star-studded cast: Woodson; Tennessee quarterback Peyton Manning; Washington State quarterback Ryan Leaf, who would face Woodson in the Rose Bowl; and Marshall wide receiver Randy Moss. All were first-round selections in the NFL draft the following spring.

Woodson's chief competition for the award was Manning, who'd returned for his senior season with the idea of winning the Heisman. He'd been on everyone's watch list since the end of the previous season. The Heisman, it appeared, was his to lose. Woodson also had to buck decades of tradition: The award typically went to the quarterback, running back, or wide receiver with the gaudiest statistics.

Manning's numbers were impressive, but no player that season affected a game in as many ways as Woodson did, and he did so in big-play fashion in big games. As Minnesota coach Glen Mason said about Woodson after his team's 24–3 loss at Michigan Stadium: "If there's a better player in the country, I don't know who he is."

Woodson turned in a highlight-film kind of season. His one-handed, sideline-straddling interception in a 23–7 win at Michigan State was the outstanding individual effort of the season. He later iced a 34–8 victory at Penn State—a triumph that vaulted Michigan into the top spot in the Associated Press "Top 25" poll—with a 37-yard touchdown reception.

As Harmon and Howard had done before him, Woodson came up even bigger in the season finale against Ohio State. He intercepted a pass in the end zone, set up Michigan's only offensive touchdown with a long reception, and broke the game open with a 78-yard punt return for a touchdown. The Wolverines earned the Big Ten title and the trip to the Rose Bowl with a 20–14 win. That performance was the clincher for many Heisman voters. One later remarked: "He did everything in that game. I kept thinking: 'Is there anything he can't do?' Woodson has done all he possibly can to show he's the best guy in the country."

He Who Laughs Last . . .

Charles Woodson exorcised his demons with a brilliant performance at Michigan State during his Heisman season.

Two seasons earlier, MSU quarterback Tony Banks had picked on Woodson, then a freshman, in leading the Spartans to a come-from-behind 28–25 win. Woodson was burned twice in the fourth quarter, once for a touchdown by Nigea Carter, then on a completion to Derrick Mason that set up the winning touchdown.

In Michigan's 23–7 win in East Lansing in 1997, the Wolverines intercepted six passes. Woodson had two of them, including an improbable grab along the Michigan sideline. Woodson leaped high in the air, reached skyward with his arm and hauled in the pass with one hand, and then came down with one foot inbounds.

"When I saw it, my heart just dropped," teammate Sam Sword recalled. "I was like, 'Oh my God!' But you know what? We expect those kind of plays from Charles."

Tennessee fans didn't agree, and they worried, with good reason, that the upstart from Michigan would steal the award that rightfully belonged to their favorite son, Manning. The suddenness of Woodson's climb to prominence gave rise to a number of conspiracy theories among Manning supporters, including some who suggested that the Heisman battle was the Civil War being fought all over again. When Woodson was announced as the winner, Tennessee governor Don Sundquist reacted angrily: "I think it stinks. I think the Heisman award has been diminished."

As Washington State's Leaf prepared to leave the Downtown Athletic Club after the trophy presentation, he reflected on what Woodson had just accomplished. "I had been focusing just on Michigan for the Rose Bowl," he said. "Now, I have to concentrate on the Heisman Trophy winner." It was a comment no one would have comprehended until that moment, because a quarterback had never before had to worry about facing a Heisman winner. Woodson had changed all that.

"For a defensive player to win this award, it's truly a breakthrough," Woodson said. "I feel like a pioneer right now."

After he returned the punt for a touchdown in the Ohio State game, Woodson appeared as if he was ready to strike the Heisman pose, as Howard had done in the same game six years earlier. Woodson never had the chance because he was swarmed by celebrating teammates.

When asked after winning the award whether he'd like to have another shot at it, Woodson said: "I'd love to strike the pose."

And he did.

Michigan's Return to Glory

The 1969 Ohio State Game

A fter concluding his remarks at a banquet in his honor several years after he finished his Ohio State coaching career, Woody Hayes was asked which of his thirty-eight teams was the best.

His 1969 team, he answered without hesitation.

With that, Hayes slowly turned and stared down the dais at his former protégé and longtime rival, Michigan coach Bo Schembechler. Following a long, uncomfortable pause, Hayes said: "Damn you, Bo, you'll never win a bigger game!"

Hayes was right. Schembechler would coach twenty-one seasons at Michigan and retire as the program's all-time winningest coach, but none of his 194 victories was more important than the stunning 24–12 upset his Wolverines pulled off his first season against the top-ranked and defending national champion Buckeyes.

In fact it has been argued that no win in the Wolverines' history was more critical—a bold statement given that Michigan is college football's winningest program. But there is little doubt that this game was a turning point in the modern history of the program.

"It really was," former Michigan All-American Dan Dierdorf recalled on the thirtieth anniversary of the game.

"Michigan had played good, but not great, football during the decade of the 1960s. The program hadn't had consistent success. It started in 1969, and that game was like a kick-starter on a motorcycle. That success is running to this day."

Schembechler guided his seventeen-point underdog Wolverines over an Ohio State team that was so formidable that one newspaper suggested the Buckeyes bypass the Rose Bowl and head right to the Super Bowl. The magnitude of the win was such that those Michigan fans who witnessed it or who were in Ann Arbor at the time were indelibly touched by it: They can remember where they were and what they were doing.

"I think it was the most important win in the history of Michigan football," former captain and All-American tight end Jim Mandich said three decades later. "It was the launch pad for years of great Michigan football. That game put Michigan back on top again. I'm not saying that as an egomaniac. It's a fact."

Cecil Pryor, a senior defensive end on the '69 team, agreed: "Most of the people who followed us, especially those immediately after, view it the same way. That was the game that started the foundation for the rebirth. Michigan had always had good football teams. We were 8–2 the year before. We were not down in the dumps, but that win more or less brought a renewed spirit to Michigan football."

After winning back-to-back national championships in 1947 and 1948, Michigan claimed just three Big Ten championships and played in two Rose

Bowls in the two decades that followed. In ten of those seasons, the Wolverines would finish fifth or worse in the Big Ten standings. The balance of power in the state had shifted from Ann Arbor to East Lansing.

"When I came to Ann Arbor in 1966, if you told people from out of state that you went to Michigan, they'd ask if you meant Michigan State," Mandich said. "It was green and white all over the place."

Not after the 1969 season. It forever changed the perception of college football in the state.

In the three decades that followed, Michigan never had a losing season. From 1969 to 2000, Michigan would win outright or share nineteen Big Ten championships, would play in

Running back Garvie Craw plows through a tackle by Ohio State's Mike Sensibaugh to score the first Michigan touchdown in a 24–12 win in 1969. (Ann Arbor News)

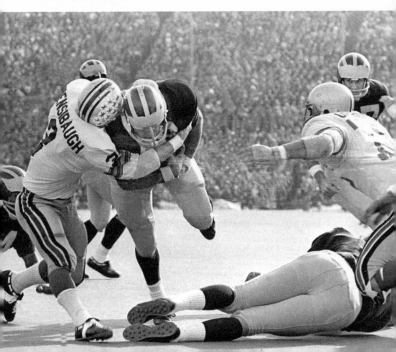

thirteen Rose Bowls, and would win a national championship. Beginning in 1975, the Wolverines would begin a consecutive bowl streak that was second only to Nebraska's. That '75 season was also the last time Michigan failed to draw at least 100,000 fans for a home game.

The catalyst for all of it was that improbable win against the Buckeyes.

"It's not often that you work hard, play hard, and get the chance to do something special like that," Dierdorf said. "I played in the NFL for twelve years. I received every honor I could receive. That '69 game was the biggest win of my football life. It was my best three hours as a football player."

The seeds for those marvelous three hours were sown a year earlier at Ohio Stadium, after the Big Ten champion Buckeyes crushed the Wolverines, 50–14. In an attempt to add to Michigan's humiliation that afternoon, Hayes elected to try for a two-point conversion after the Buckeyes' final touchdown. It failed, but no Wolverine would ever forget it.

"That game was a fiasco," Dierdorf recalled. "I was a sophomore and the starting right tackle, and I tore up my knee in the game. I had to watch from the sidelines. I remember being in the locker room [for treatment] and feeling the stadium just shake. Before I could get back out on the field, the locker room shook again. That was humiliating."

After the game Mandich and Pryor assembled the team's underclassmen on one bus. During the long bus ride back to Ann Arbor, the Wolverines pledged that the Buckeyes would not win the following season in Michigan Stadium. What the players didn't know then was that they would play that next game against the Buckeyes under a new head coach.

Schembechler, like Fielding Yost and Fritz Crisler before him, did not have a "Michigan" pedigree. He was an all-state lineman from Barberton, Ohio, who went on to play college football for Hayes at Miami of Ohio. He would earn a master's degree at Ohio State, where he was a member of Hayes's coaching staff. He would serve as an assistant coach in three college programs before returning to his alma mater in 1963. His 40–17–3 record at Miami in six seasons would eventually get Michigan's attention.

Interestingly, Schembechler was not Michigan athletic director Don Canham's first choice to replace Bump Elliott. Canham first interviewed Joe Paterno, who'd been the Penn State head coach for three seasons. Paterno was flattered to be offered the job, but he turned down Canham because it would have meant abandoning his team before it played in its bowl game that season. Two days later, Canham called again, this

Legendary Ohio State coach Woody Hayes, whose 1969 undefeated team was upset by Michigan in the season finale, 24–12 (Ann Arbor News)

time to ask Paterno if he knew anything about Miami of Ohio's coach, a guy named Schembechler. Paterno didn't, but he recalled that Hayes once told him he considered Schembechler one of the young coaches he'd recommend for a big-time job. That was enough for Canham.

Compared with the low-key, personable Elliott, the intense Schembechler was like a cold slap in the face. After arriving in Ann Arbor in early 1969, he began reshaping the Wolverines into a team that mirrored his personality. "Bo was a guy who had a plan for everything, and he had a plan for Ohio State that went back to his first day on campus," former Michigan fullback Fritz Seyferth recalled. "He knew that to get credibility, that was the program you had to beat. The reality was, he had to beat them."

Dierdorf found out his new head coach meant business the first time he met him. During his high school playing days in Canton, Ohio, Dierdorf had been recruited by Miami of Ohio, among many others, but he elected early on to attend Michigan. Once, when then-Miami assistant Jerry Hanlon stopped by his high school for a scheduled visit, Dierdorf blew off the appointment, figuring he'd never see Hanlon again. Not long after Schembechler (and Hanlon) arrived in Ann Arbor, Dierdorf decided he'd better make some sort of apology for his bad manners. On meeting Schembechler, Dierdorf offered a handshake. Schembechler brushed it aside and instead grabbed a handful of Dierdorf's gut. Looking Dierdorf directly in the eye, Schembechler said: "You're fat, you're mine, and I never forget!"

In previous seasons players had been allowed to lift weights on their own and play basketball at the IM Building to stay in shape. Now, with Schembechler and his coaches supervising, workouts became more structured and intense. "What he put us through was more demanding than anything I've been through, before or since," Pryor recalled. "Our winter workouts went from being good to being a total nightmare."

Pryor recalled that the Wolverines used to do a drill called "Slap Stomp" in the boxing ring of the basement of the IM Building. Players would stomp on one another's feet and then slap the other guy from the neck on down. Pryor said he suspected the drill was supposed to enhance quickness, but he still believed it was stupid. When a teammate slapped him in the face once by accident, his instinctive reaction was to punch him. "I'd yell at [Bo], and he'd yell at me," Pryor recalled. "Then he'd kick me off the team and eventually let me back on. I thought he was completely mad. After the winter conditioning program, we all thought he was mad."

Schembechler's demanding regimen scared off many players, but those who stayed said they did so because they found in their new head coach both a disciplinarian who set an example with his own work ethic and a coach who shared their desire to return Michigan to its place among the nation's elite programs. At one point during that first tough spring, as player after player was leaving the team, Schembechler coined a slogan, "Those Who Stay Will Be Champions," and hung it over the entrance to the locker room. It is still one of the mantras of the Michigan football program.

"I'm not exactly sure why, but the '69 team has a special bond," Dierdorf said. "Our motto was: 'We stayed!' We survived this tornado [Schembechler] that blew into Ann Arbor."

Michigan started the season 3–2, with early losses to Missouri and Michigan State, but it rolled into the Ohio State game with lopsided wins against Minnesota, Wisconsin, Illinois, and Iowa. The Wolverines were so charged up after a 51–6 win at Iowa on the next-to-last weekend of the season that they were prepared to take on the Buckeyes right then.

"Even though no one gave us a chance, we knew we would win," Mandich said. "I will never forget the scene in the locker room at Iowa. It was bedlam. If they could have flown Ohio State into Iowa City at that moment, we would have gone another sixty minutes. That was what our whole mentality was about."

Dierdorf said he will never forget the scene in the visitors' locker room after the Iowa game. "There was no celebration," he recalled. "It was just a pedal-to-the-metal eruption. We were all saying, 'Give us Ohio State!' It was one of the more remarkable things I have ever been around."

Following the most intense week of practice any of the players could remember, the Wolverines were primed to explode. Schembechler made certain his players did not forget the humiliation of the previous season. He had the number "50" painted on everything, including the helmets and uniforms of players running the demonstration teams.

"Bo will tell you the fever pitch started on Tuesday and never went down," former Michigan offensive lineman Dick Caldarazzo said. "He didn't have to say anything, and he didn't seem to worry that we'd hit a peak. He'd say, 'Heck, let 'em keep going.' Our scrimmages were ridiculous."

Pryor agreed: "Everyone was focused. We all had a bad attitude, but it was not negative. It was real intense and edgy and focused. You could tell by the number of skirmishes and scuffles. There were a lot of them."

By mid-November, Ohio State was being hailed in the national media as one of the greatest college teams of all time. Journalists used words like "unbeatable" and "invincible" to describe the Buckeyes. Hayes's team arrived in Ann Arbor riding a twenty-two-game winning streak. It had annihilated every opponent it had faced that season. The narrowest margin of victory was twenty-seven points. Oddsmakers expected more of the same in the season finale.

When Schembechler led his team into Michigan Stadium that Saturday for pregame warm-ups, he encountered Hayes and the Buckeyes already out there warming up—on Michigan's end of the field. Hayes had decided to test the mettle of his protégé, and Schembechler answered the challenge. He instructed his players to take their rightful places on the field. Then, he walked up to Hayes and said, "Coach, you are warming up on the wrong side of the field." Hayes grumbled, then motioned to his players to move to the other end of the field. The Michigan players went wild.

There was a similar confrontation in the tunnel right before the game, but this one didn't end peacefully. The Buckeyes had left their locker room early and blocked the Wolverines in their attempt to run onto the field. When the Wolverines pushed their way through, the teams scuffled. During the brief altercation, Pryor punched Ohio State quarterback Rex Kern and yanked off his helmet. Later, it was reported that Pryor attempted to shove Kern through the door to the visitors' locker room. Pryor said that never happened.

"Needless to say, that set the tone for the day," Pryor said. "They were the reigning national champions, and they acted the part. They disrespected us totally. That [fight] set the tone for the day. We had the police and referees break things up. It was quite a scene. Knowing Bo, he might have got a punch or two in, too."

On the first play of Ohio State's first possession, the Buckeyes broke a sweep around Pryor's end for 20 yards. He'd screwed up so badly he began to question himself. But, after getting over the shock of the first play, he quickly settled down and so did the Wolverines. Fullback Jim Otis scored on the

Buckeyes' second drive to give Ohio State a 6–0 lead. The extra-point attempt failed. The Wolverines answered on their next possession, driving 55 yards to set up a 1-yard touchdown run by Garvie Craw. Frank Titas's extra point gave Michigan a 7–6 lead.

"We stuffed the ball down their throats on that drive," Caldarazzo recalled. "It was the first time they'd been in a drive like that all season. You could see [Jim] Stillwagon and Doug Adams. They were flushed and sweating bullets. They were wondering what was happening, because they had clobbered everyone. Right then, all the linemen knew we had a great chance to beat them."

The Buckeyes took a 12–7 lead eight seconds into the second quarter on a 22-yard touchdown pass from Kern to Jan White. White kicked the extra point, but Michigan was penalized half the distance to the goal line on the play. The Buckeyes elected to try for two points. Kern wanted to pass, but he never got the chance. Michigan's Mike Keller sacked him.

Glen Doughty's 31-yard return of the ensuing kickoff gave Michigan the ball at its 42 yard line. Six plays later, including a brilliant broken-field run of 28 yards by Billy Taylor, Craw scored again from the 1 yard line. Titas's kick gave the Wolverines a 14–12 lead.

"As I look back on it now, the team fed off the enthusiasm of the crowd," Craw said. "We were prepared to play that game as any team can be, emotionally and physically."

Then came the turning point. The Buckeyes were forced to punt, and Barry Pierson returned the ball 60 yards before being knocked out of bounds at the Ohio State 3. Two plays later, quarterback Don Moorhead dove into the end zone from 2 yards out. Later, with 1:15 remaining in the first half, Tim Killian kicked a 25-yard field goal. That was all the scoring for the afternoon.

Michigan's Barry Pierson (29) cuts upfield behind Bruce Elliott (21) during his 60-yard punt return against Ohio State in 1969. (Ann Arbor News)

The Michigan defense turned in an inspired effort in the second half. The Wolverines' defensive line shut down Ohio State's powerful option attack, forcing the Buckeyes into the unfamiliar and uncomfortable position of having to throw the ball. Pierson intercepted three passes, and Tom Curtis picked off two.

Statistically, the game was much closer than the outcome. Michigan held a slim advantage in first downs (21–20) and total yards (374–373). Moorhead connected on ten of his twenty pass attempts for 108 yards. Mandich caught six passes for 78 yards. Kern completed only ten of his twenty-eight pass attempts for 108 yards. He was intercepted six times.

When the game ended, deliriously happy Michigan fans swarmed the field. The field was jammed long after the two teams retreated to their respective locker rooms.

"I'll never forget being in the locker room after the game," Caldarazzo said. "Every guy was exhausted, even the ones who hadn't played a lick. Everyone had given everything he had. It meant so much to all of us. Going to the Rose Bowl was an afterthought at that point."

The victory was the 517th in Michigan history and very likely the sweetest ever. The loss was the 198th in Ohio State history, and it was, judging from Hayes's later comments, one of the most bitter and disappointing. The Buckeyes returned to Columbus and called it a season. Michigan, which shared the Big Ten championship with Ohio State, went to the Rose Bowl to face Southern Cal.

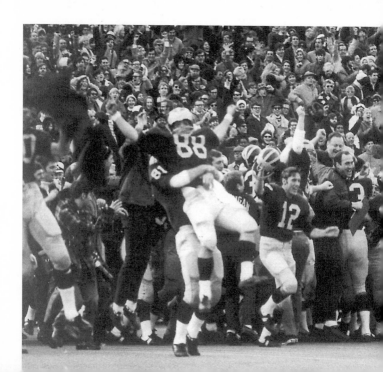

That game would not have a happy ending. The night before the game, Schembechler suffered a heart attack and was eventually taken to the hospital. Stunned, the Wolverines lost to the Trojans, 10–3. It was Michigan's first loss in the Rose Bowl.

That defeat did not diminish the feeling of accomplishment among the players on Schembechler's first team. And nothing could detract from the shocking win against Ohio State.

"We feel very proud that we were the team that is looked upon as putting the Michigan program back on the map," Craw said. "There were a lot of games played before 1969, and Michigan will play a lot of games in the future. Michigan football is bigger than any one game, but that one sort of defines our careers. That game pushed Michigan into the winning modern era."

The Michigan bench erupts at the conclusion of the Wolverines' 24–12 win against top-ranked Ohio State in 1969.
(Bentley Historical Library)

As he looked back on the game from the perspective of three decades, Dierdorf is still amazed at what he and his teammates accomplished that late November afternoon.

"All I think of is, what a great team we beat," he said. "That was one of the greatest teams ever assembled. We were not. But I look at that achievement—and I think this is where a lot of the cohesiveness of that team comes from—we were not the most talented team, but we proved why you bother to play the game. We were seventeen-point underdogs, but it didn't matter. We not only won, but Ohio State knew we won.

"We know—and this is one of the sources of pride for that team—that we were partly responsible for the resurrection of Michigan football. We started a run that continues to this day."

The 1969 Season

Date	Opponent	Result
September 20	vs. Vanderbilt	W, 42–14
September 27	vs. Washington	W, 45–7
October 4	vs. Missouri	L, 40–17
October 11	vs. Purdue	W, 31–20
October 18	at Michigan State	L, 23–12
October 25	at Minnesota	W, 35–9
November 1	vs. Wisconsin	W, 35–7
November 8	at Illinois	W, 57–0
November 15	at Iowa	W, 51–6
November 22	vs. Ohio State	W, 24–12

The Top 10 Michigan Football Games of the Twentieth Century

1. **1969 vs. Ohio State:** In the game that sets the tone for Bo Schembechler's tenure as head coach, Michigan stuns the defending national champions, 24–12.

2. **1998 Rose Bowl:** Led by bowl MVP Brian Griese and Heisman Trophy winner Charles Woodson, a 21–16 win against Washington State gives Michigan its first national championship in five decades.

3. **1948 Rose Bowl:** In Fritz Crisler's final game as head coach, Michigan overpowers Southern Cal, 49–0. Bob Chappuis, who plays with a sore hamstring, is the game's MVP.

4. **1902 Rose Bowl:** Michigan wins the first Rose Bowl ever played, 49–0 against Stanford. Neil Snow scores five touchdowns in a game that was ended at Stanford's request with eight minutes remaining.

5. **1950 at Ohio State:** In "The Snow Bowl," Michigan pulls out a 9–3 win to clinch a bid to the Rose Bowl. The game, played in whiteout snow conditions, features a record forty-five punts between the two teams, including one that is blocked and recovered for the winning touchdown by Michigan's Tony Momsen.

6. **1942 at Notre Dame:** In the first meeting between the two teams since 1909, the sixth-ranked Wolverines post a 33–20 win against the number four Fighting Irish.

7. **1997 at Penn State:** Ranked number four heading into the weekend, the Wolverines vault into first place in the Associated Press poll with a convincing 34–8 win against the second-ranked Nittany Lions.

8. **1940 at Ohio State:** In his final college game eventual Heisman winner Tom Harmon earns a standing ovation from the Ohio Stadium crowd with a brilliant performance. He runs for 139 yards and two touchdowns, completes eleven of twelve passes for 151 yards and two touchdowns, intercepts three passes (returning one for a touchdown), and averages 50 yards a punt. Michigan wins, 40–0.

9. **1981 Rose Bowl:** The Wolverines hand Schembechler his first bowl win in convincing fashion, 23–6 against Washington.

10. **1994 vs. Colorado:** The game features what is arguably the most memorable play of the decade, a 64-yard "Hail Mary" touchdown pass from Kordell Stewart to Michael Westbrook on the game's final play to give Colorado a 27–26 win.

A First for Bo

The 1981 Rose Bowl Champions

B o Schembechler was late. It was only minutes, but that was enough to get his players' attention. The Michigan coach was nothing if not punctual. He would arrive for the weekly Sunday afternoon full-team meeting promptly at 2:59. The doors closed at 3:01. No player dared walk in late. It was better to miss one of those meetings altogether and deal with Schembechler's anger later, players recalled, than to bear the brunt of it immediately in front of teammates.

On this Sunday afternoon in late September 1980, every Wolverine was present. No one was willing to risk the head coach's wrath, not after one of the most gut-wrenching defeats in program history. The afternoon before in South Bend, Indiana, Notre Dame kicker Harry Oliver had accomplished the improbable, booting a career-best 51-yard field goal on the game's final play to stun the Wolverines, 29–27. That wasn't all. The week before, the Wolverines had barely hung on to defeat lowly Northwestern, 17–10, in the season opener. Coupled with three consecutive losses to conclude the 1979 season, the Wolverines were in a funk neither they nor Schembechler had ever experienced.

Three o'clock came. No Schembechler. No assistant coaches. The players looked at each other nervously. Five minutes passed. Still no coaches. "Bo was never late," running back Stanley Edwards recalled. "He was like clockwork. Everyone could feel the tension."

At 3:10 Schembechler marched into the room and immediately dispatched the defensive players to another meeting room. He then informed the offensive players that he had decided to abandon the option that had been the program's staple since he'd arrived from Miami of Ohio more than a decade earlier. The Wolverines simply weren't moving the ball that way, he said. Michigan was going to a power running attack.

"To be into the season and to scrap the offense, to throw it out the window, that was scary, but it was also a little exciting," Edwards said. "In my mind it was unprecedented for Bo to admit that he was wrong."

Other players interpreted the change differently: not as an admission of failure, but as yet another sign of his genius as a head coach. Schembechler's decision to make a change, even after the season had begun, was simply a recognition that Michigan's personnel was better suited for a different style of play, one that would steamroll opponents rather than attempt to deceive them.

Schembechler possessed all the ingredients he needed for a power running game: a veteran offense line, a trio of outstanding running backs, an experienced and confident quarterback, and a game-breaking wide receiver who many Michigan fans still contend is the finest player ever to wear the winged helmet. It was simply a matter of the coach recognizing what he had.

"We had a lot of confidence in Bo," center and cocaptain George Lilja said. "In making this change we were behind him. We knew he had put a lot of thought into it. I'm sure there had been a lot of discussion among the coaches. We can only speculate how much. But he made the decision, and it turned out to be the right one."

It did, but not immediately. Michigan's funk continued a week later when the Wolverines played South Carolina at Michigan Stadium. The Wolverines jumped out to a 14–0 lead and missed a chance to make it 21–0 when Edwards fumbled into the end zone. That gave the Gamecocks, led by eventual Heisman Trophy winner George Rogers, the opportunity they needed to get back into the game and eventually win it. South Carolina's 17–14 victory dropped the Wolverines to 1–2 and out of the national rankings for the first time since 1969, Schembechler's first season. Michigan had lost five of its last six games. One national publication, which ranked the worst teams in college football, listed the Wolverines at number two. The program, it appeared, had hit a crossroads.

"We could very well have been 0–3," linebacker Mel Owens said. "Climbing out of that hole would have been near impossible. Now, we were in a position of just trying to salvage the season. It looked like the start of a bad stretch for Michigan. And I just kept thinking: 'It's my last year. I don't want it to end this way.' "

That it didn't end badly was a tribute to Lilja, fellow captain Andy Cannavino, and the team's other seniors, such as Owens and quarterback John Wangler. It also was a tribute to the tradition of the program. This group of Wolverines did not want to be the first of Schembechler's teams to suffer a losing season. Rather, they wanted to be remembered for turning adversity into success. They would do just that, and, ultimately, they would accomplish one more thing: They would give Schembechler his first Rose Bowl victory.

"We could have tanked and went under," Lilja said. "But we all got together after the South Carolina game, and we decided that we had too much character, too much talent to let this thing slip away. We were going to do all we could to turn it around."

At some point early in the season, defensive coordinator Bill McCartney asked Cannavino what the players were thinking about the way Schembechler was handling the team. It was not an unusual question, Cannavino said, because players were on a first-name basis with the assistants. Cannavino leveled with McCartney: Players were telling him they believed Schembechler's three-hour practices were wearing them out. McCartney relayed the conversation to Schembechler, who called Cannavino on the carpet, demanding to know how a captain could think that way. The coach's message to his seniors was simple: Stop whining and start leading.

"People thought I was complaining, but I had just told him what the guys were saying," Cannavino recalled. "But I really became a better leader after that. One time, Mike Trgovac ran into the huddle late and wanted to know the play. I told him that if he didn't know the play, he should get the hell out of there. He was my best friend, and people were shocked that I would say something like that. [But] that's how I approached things. We were like coaches on the field. I was so intense and so into it, and I wanted to win so bad. We all became better leaders. It was the little things that made the difference."

The truth is, the last senior Schembechler needed to take to task for a lack of leadership was Cannavino. Every player's one enduring memory of the season is of an exhausted Cannavino sprawled in the aisle of the team's charter plane on the ride home from Notre Dame. Dehydrated, he had an IV in his arm. He could not sit in his seat because he was cramping so badly. When the team got back to Ann Arbor, he weighed himself. He'd lost eighteen pounds during the game. "I'm not sure if seeing me on the plane helped the team, but I think my

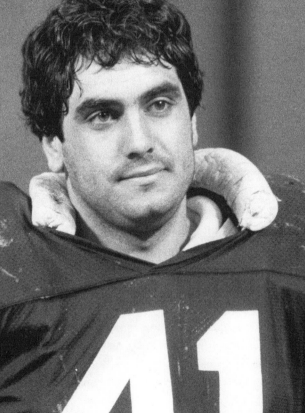

Linebacker Andy Cannavino, one of the captains of the 1980 team that won the Big Ten championship and gave Coach Bo Schembechler his first Rose Bowl victory.
(Ann Arbor News)

effort might have rubbed off on the younger guys," Cannavino said. "When you live through it, you don't think about it, but I was spent. Maybe the younger guys wanted to go to the extra mile after they saw that."

Schembechler demonstrated in the South Carolina loss that he had little confidence in his defense, and it cost the team dearly. Rather than let his defense try to protect a slim lead, Schembechler elected to try a fake punt. It might not have been a bad call in the South Carolina end of the field, but the Wolverines were in their own territory. The play was stopped, and the defense wound up on the field in a whole lot worse shape than it would have been had the Wolverines punted. The Gamecocks capitalized to take the lead. Owens said Michigan's defensive players, their pride badly hurt, demanded that Schembechler make a decision: Either he trusted them, or he didn't. Schembechler promised never to doubt them again.

But the coach also made certain that he would never again have reason to doubt his defense. Schembechler and McCartney made a change in practice that would help to turn the defense into a ferocious unit, one that ultimately would earn the nickname "McCartney's Monsters." Practice drills typically pitted the number one offense and the number one defense against demonstration teams, not against each other, but Schembechler decided his young defense needed as much exposure to game-type situations as it could get. So, during a drill called "full line," the defensive front seven faced the offensive line and running backs. There was no passing, just running between the tackles. The defense waged an all-out war against one of the best offensive lines and some of the best running backs in the nation. The improvement was dramatic, because nothing the defense would see on a Saturday afternoon compared with what they faced every day in practice. Just as important, the intense drill set an enthusiastic tone for practice. Players insist the team never had a bad practice again after Schembechler made the change to "full line." The Wolverines were ready to make a run at the Big Ten championship.

Wangler had been the starting quarterback at the end of the 1979 season, but he'd suffered a serious knee injury in the Gator Bowl game against North Carolina, when he was tackled by Lawrence Taylor. Recognizing that the 1980 season would be his last, Wangler spent many hours each day during the off-season rehabilitating the knee enough so that he might be able to play. When summer practice began, he was still not 100 percent and certainly not mobile enough to run the option. Sophomore Rich Hewlett started against Northwestern and Notre Dame, but after the Fighting Irish jumped out to a 14–0 lead in the second quarter of that game, Schembechler asked Wangler if he could go. Wangler said he could, and Schembechler told him not to worry about anything other than throwing the ball. Schembechler then instructed the members of his offensive line that no Notre Dame defender was to lay a hand on Wangler. None did, and Wangler led one of the gutsiest comebacks in program history. Wangler took over with 4:53 remaining in the first half. With less than a minute remaining before intermission, the score was tied at 14–all.

"The Notre Dame game was significant, not for the way we lost, but for the way we came back," Wangler said. "I'll tell you what, I was not hit a lot that season. I was maybe sacked twelve times. The offensive line was tremendous, and Bo and Mo (offensive coordinator Gary Moeller) put me in a position to do what I could do. Plus, we had the kind of a running game that took the pressure off the quarterback."

The offensive line was imposing. Lilja, guard Kurt Becker and tackles Ed Muransky and Bubba Paris all would go on to

Ahead of His Time

The 1980 Michigan defense, which did not give up a touchdown in the final twenty-two quarters of the season, was nicknamed "McCartney's Monsters" in tribute to defensive coordinator Bill McCartney.

"We had total confidence in Coach McCartney," linebacker and senior cocaptain Andy Cannavino recalled. "No matter what defense he called in games down the stretch, we knew we would shut teams down."

Cannavino believes McCartney might have been the first defensive coordinator to use a "dime" package for pass coverage, employing six defensive backs in an effort to stop Purdue quarterback Mark Herrmann in the season's home finale. With only four down linemen and Cannavino in the middle, the Wolverines dared Purdue to run the ball. The Boilermakers couldn't and finished with only 50 yards rushing. Herrmann, who'd been averaging 320 passing yards a game, threw for 129 against Michigan. The Wolverines won, 26–0.

"McCartney was an innovator," Cannavino said. "This was the first time Michigan had ever done anything like that. No one had ever heard about the 'dime' before. I thought that was pretty cool."

play in the NFL. Guard John Powers and tight end Norm Betts could have played pro football but chose not to. The running backs—Edwards, Butch Woolfolk, and Lawrence Ricks—were as good a trio as Michigan has ever possessed. The Wolverines, who failed to run the ball consistently using the option, wound up leading the nation in rushing that season, averaging 251.9 yards a game. Woolfolk, who averaged 5.3 yards per carry, finished with 1,042 yards. The Wolverines averaged 140.3 passing yards, but the threat of the pass kept defenses constantly on edge. Wangler was a marvelous passer who threw what Edwards described as the most catchable ball he'd ever seen. His favorite receiver was sophomore wide receiver Anthony Carter, whose explosiveness and elusiveness would drive defenders crazy for four seasons. Carter caught fifty-one passes in 1980, the most in any one season during his Michigan career.

Schembechler's decision to change gave Michigan the ability to possess the ball for long stretches of time, which kept the defense off the field and rested. Typically, the defense would then force an opponent to go three and out, and the offense would put together another relentless march down the field. Games became wars of attrition that only the Wolverines could win.

Michigan rebounded from the South Carolina loss with a big win against California, but the Wolverines barely got by Michigan State at home, 27–23, when Big Ten play resumed in October. That was as close as any opponent would get to the Wolverines the rest of the season. Michigan kept the Little Brown Jug with a 37–14 win at Minnesota and then blasted Illinois, 45–14, for homecoming.

The Illinois game was a personal turning point for Owens, who played outside linebacker. Fighting Illini quarterback Dave Wilson picked on Owens with short patterns to the backs and tight ends during the first half. Owens struggled so badly that after one series, McCartney told him he was going to stop calling certain defenses because Owens couldn't play the coverage. Owens was stunned and angered at being called out by his coach. He told McCartney that he would get the job done, no matter what it took. "My game went up mentally at that point," Owens said.

Coincidentally, Michigan's defensive play went up at that point, too. The two touchdowns scored by the Illini in the first half would be the last the Wolverines would give up that season. They shut out Indiana, Wisconsin, and Purdue; gave up a field goal to Ohio State; and allowed Washington two field goals in the Rose Bowl. Down the stretch, the Wolverines went twenty-two consecutive quarters without giving up a touchdown. The defense's confidence was sky high. During warm-ups before the November 8 game at Wisconsin, Schembechler told Owens he didn't think the Wolverines were ready to play. Owens replied that the coach had nothing to worry about, that the defense was posting nothing but shutouts from that point on, and that the team was going to run the table.

The defense delivered its most brilliant performance in the November 13 home finale against Purdue. The Boilermakers, led by the superb passing of Mark Herrmann, averaged forty-two points, 320 passing yards, 222 rushing yards, five touchdowns, and 27.2 first downs a game. They needed a win to wrap up a trip to the Rose Bowl. Purdue's offense was no match for Michigan's rugged defense. The Boilermakers finished with 50 yards rushing, and Herrmann, who was hounded constantly, passed for just 129 yards. Michigan rolled to a 26–0 win that vaulted the team back into the nation's top ten. "We just beat the heck out of them," Cannavino said. "It was our last home game. We had so much confidence, and we were so excited. We knew they couldn't run the ball on us."

or the thirteenth consecutive season, the Big Ten champi-
and Rose Bowl representative was decided in the
higan–Ohio State game. The previous season in Ann Arbor,
Buckeyes had blocked a punt for the winning touchdown in
18–15 triumph. The Michigan defense was the difference in
lumbus, as the Wolverines posted a 9–3 victory. Ali Haji-
heikh's 43-yard field goal and Wangler's 13-yard touchdown
ass to Carter in the third quarter accounted for all the Michigan
scoring. It was more than enough. "We all wanted to win that
game so much," Betts recalled. "To beat them at Ohio State . . .
I remember the feeling. The adrenaline buzz still comes back to
me now. We wanted to beat them bad and go to the Rose Bowl."

The Wolverines headed to Pasadena determined to give
Schembechler his first bowl victory. Most upperclassmen were
making their third trip to the Rose Bowl, where they had only
known disappointment. This time, they said, it would be different. Bowl preparation definitely was different. In previous seasons, because there was no indoor practice facility in Ann
Arbor, Schembechler took the team to the bowl site before
Christmas and worked the players so hard that some suggested
a bowl trip was a punishment rather than a reward. But the
Wolverines' new indoor field house was completed just in time
for bowl practice, so Schembechler kept the team in Ann Arbor
until Christmas Day. Just as important, he limited practices to
one each day. Consequently, the Wolverines were in excellent
spirits and shape to face Washington on New Year's Day.

"I think in the back of our minds, maybe early on, we'd
remember we were on the West Coast, and Michigan teams
weren't supposed to win there," Edwards said. "But halfway
through the game, we started to realize this was our game. We
started to own them in the third and fourth quarter. We were
about to make history and become Bo's first bowl winner. I

Butch Woolfolk (24) busts through the Washington defensive line on his 6-yard touchdown run in the 1981 Rose Bowl. Woolfolk, who rushed for 186 yards, was named the player of the game. (Bentley Historical Library)

think Bo had more confidence than we did. He felt this was the team, that it could beat anyone. None of us had ever been on a team that good before."

Washington would compile more total yards, 374, against the Michigan defense than any team had all season, but the Huskies still could not crack the end zone. They had a chance on their second drive, when they drove to the Michigan 1 yard line, but the Wolverines stopped tailback Touissant Tyler on fourth down and seized the momentum. Michigan sandwiched a 6-yard touchdown run by Woolfolk in the second quarter between a pair of Chuck Nelson field goals for a 7–6 half-time lead. Schembechler was as calm in the locker room at intermission as any player could remember seeing him. He told his players they would win, and then he and his coaches set about making the adjustments to help them do it.

Quarterback John Wangler (5) hands off to running back Stanley Edwards (32) during Michigan's 23–6 victory over Washington in the 1981 Rose Bowl. The win was Coach Bo Schembechler's first in a bowl game.
(Bentley Historical Library)

Haji-Sheikh kicked a 25-yard field goal, and Wangler hit Carter on a 7-yard touchdown pass in the third quarter, but the Wolverines became convinced the game was theirs on one play. Facing third and 23 in Michigan territory, Schembechler called for the sprint draw. The line opened a gaping hole in the Washington defensive front, and Woolfolk blasted through it for a first down. Following that big play, the Wolverines could see the Huskies were a beaten team. Edwards capped the scoring in fourth quarter with a 1-yard touchdown run. Michigan had a 23–6 victory. Woolfolk was voted the game's outstanding player after rushing for 182 yards.

"That game was something special," Wangler said. "It was like the weight of the world was lifted off our backs. To see Bo as happy as he was, to know how far we had come that season, to finally be able to leave a season winning our last game, we did not want it to end. We had paid our dues. We hung in there. Nothing came easy, but to win that game for all the guys who'd never been able to do it, that meant a lot."

During a pep rally the afternoon before the game, Michigan radio announcer Bob Ufer told the team that they would gather in fifteen years and remember their experience in Pasadena, they would be shaking hands with their Rose Bowl championship rings, and they would remember what it took to get there. Ironically, the team did not arrange a ten-year reunion, so the next time the players gathered as a team was for the fifteenth anniversary of the season. During the reunion someone popped in a tape of Ufer's pep rally speech. To a man the players were stunned to hear Ufer mention the fifteen years. They had all forgotten he'd said it.

"His speech was prophetic," Lilja said. "It was quite a year, and it was quite a team."

The 1980 Season

Date	Opponent	Result
September 13	vs. Northwestern	W, 17–10
September 20	at Notre Dame	L, 29–27
September 27	vs. South Carolina	L, 17–14
October 4	vs. California	W, 38–13
October 11	vs. Michigan St.	W, 27–23
October 18	at Minnesota	W, 37–14
October 25	vs. Illinois	W, 45–14
November 1	at Indiana	W, 35–0
November 8	at Wisconsin	W, 24–0
November 15	vs. Purdue	W, 26–0
November 22	at Ohio State	W, 9–3
January 1	vs. Washington	W, 23–6

Mediocre No More

Michigan's 1997 National Champions

There was no disputing the evidence: Michigan hadn't won a national football championship in five decades, hadn't won a Big Ten championship in five seasons, hadn't won a bowl game in two seasons, and had just endured its fourth consecutive four-loss season.

So, it was difficult to argue with the conclusion: The once-proud Michigan block "M" had come to stand for mediocrity. At least that's what college football observers believed about the program heading into the 1997 season.

The Wolverines, it appeared, had hit a crossroads. Could third-year coach Lloyd Carr and his players return the program to the greatness of Fielding Yost, Fritz Crisler, and Bo Schembechler, or was Michigan slowly but surely slipping into obscurity?

One national publication, *The Sporting News*, concluded the latter. The publication's '97 preseason magazine—which had tabbed Michigan's first opponent, Colorado, as the favorite to win the national championship—contained a scathing article that detailed the perceived demise of the Wolverines. What it said, simply, was that the Michigan winged helmet, one of the most recognized icons in college football, no longer intimidated any opponent.

"It's really irritating to hear people say that stuff," senior running back Chris Howard said after the Wolverines crushed Colorado, 27–3, in the opener. "I'm sick and tired of it, but I also know we brought most of that on ourselves. We haven't totally dominated opponents the way Nebraska and Florida have. The good teams do that. We wanted to show that we can, too."

And the Wolverines did—all season long. Inspired by a brilliant defense that featured eventual Heisman Trophy winner Charles Woodson, Michigan would win more games (12) than any team in program history and earn three of the four national championship trophies awarded that season. Most important of all, the Wolverines returned their proud program to what Yost would have said was Michigan's rightful place in college football—the top.

"I've read where Michigan never wins national championships because that isn't their goal," Coach Carr said after the season. "In terms of the program, we always talk in terms of being the best. We've had some teams set their goals that way—winning the national championship—but this team was first of all determined to get away from four-loss seasons.

"We understood that what spoiled our [1996] season was losing a couple of games we were not prepared to play. What motivated the players in terms of goals was an understanding that they had to be ready to play each week. They understood that focus and concentration on a weekly basis would give them consistency and a chance to win more games."

The Wolverines drew their motivation and determination that season from two sources.

The first was their own failure. Michigan players were most haunted by a 9–3 loss at Purdue in the ninth game of the 1996 season that knocked them out of the Big Ten championship picture. The Wolverines, who had climbed back into the title chase the previous week with a win against Michigan State, had not been prepared to play at a championship level when they faced the Boilermakers. That defeat became one of the rallying cries for the '97 team, and the Wolverines taped the word *Purdue* over the entrance to every team meeting room as a reminder that nothing could be taken for granted.

Carr added the second critical element the summer before the season. Knowing that his team faced what the NCAA rated as the nation's most difficult schedule, Carr challenged his players to take each game as another step up a high mountain. Carr got the idea after reading Jon Krakauer's best-seller *Into Thin Air*, about a tragic attempt to scale Mount Everest. Carr asked Lou Kasischke, a resident of nearby Bloomfield Hills and one of the survivors of that Everest expedition, to speak to the team during the summer. Kasischke kept the Wolverines on the edge of their seats for more than ninety minutes.

"I don't know that it was any great theme, but it did serve as a metaphor for our season," Carr said before the Wolverines faced Washington State in the 1998 Rose Bowl. "There are a lot of things that are significant in terms of achieving a great goal in football and in climbing the highest mountain in the world. The preparation and concentration that was required each week was very important to our success."

After Kasischke's talk, Carr gave each Wolverine a climbing pick inscribed with the player's name and color-coded by class and position. The picks were then stuck into the ceiling of the team's main meeting room at Schembechler Hall to symbolize the struggle to get to the top and as a reminder of the individual and team efforts needed to achieve that goal.

Not surprisingly, each player put aside individual goals for the sake of the team. Some sacrificed more than others. Two were noteworthy: Fifth-year senior Zach Adami switched from right guard to center—a move that ultimately hurt his stock in terms of the National Football League draft—to help stabilize and provide leadership for a young offensive line. Classmate Chris Floyd, who had been recruited as a tailback, moved to fullback and emerged as one of the finest blockers in school history.

"There's something special . . . a little gift hidden in this team," junior defensive back Marcus Ray said. "It's just a feeling we have, especially about the defense. Everybody has accepted his role. The only thing anyone cares about is winning." Interestingly, Ray made that observation, not at the end of the season, but after the season opener. He recognized then that this team was something special.

Ray was right on the money, too, about the defense, which was the cornerstone of the Wolverines' success. It would be compared favorably by former Wolverines with some of the finest units the program had ever produced.

The defense led the Big Ten in every team statistical category and the nation in most of them. The Wolverines gave up 8.9 points a game during the regular season, the nation's lowest total since Auburn allowed 7.2 points a game in 1988. They allowed an average of 206.9 total yards a game, the lowest total since Alabama allowed 194.2 yards in 1992.

The foundation for that championship defense was built the previous season. The architect was assistant coach Jim Herrmann, who was named defensive coordinator before the 1997 Outback Bowl against Alabama. Herrmann built an attacking defense around two veterans, Woodson and senior defensive end Glen Steele. Woodson, a junior who would become the first primarily defensive player to win the Heisman, was so feared as a cornerback that most opposing offenses avoided throwing anywhere in his direction. Steele was so strong against the run and such a relentless pass rusher that opponents had to account for him with two and sometimes three blockers. That usually freed up his younger linemates, such as Josh Williams and Rob Renes, to make big plays.

But Herrmann, a former Michigan linebacker himself, believed that the defense was successful because eleven guys played as one. That, he said, was what had always epitomized "Michigan defense." "It's not one guy here or one superstar there," he said in accepting the Broyles Award that season as the nation's top assistant coach. "It's eleven guys who work in unison and who go after the football with reckless abandon. When I say 'Michigan defense,' that's what I envision. I see eleven winged helmets knocking the heck out of somebody."

The defense was never better that season than it was in preserving a 21–14 win against Notre Dame in September. Three times following turnovers in its own territory in the fourth quarter, the defense was asked to protect the slim lead. Each time, the defense answered the call. "To turn the ball over three times . . . we were facing a loss, or at least overtime," Carr said. "But the guys on defense, they were just tremendous. They hung together and fought like the devil."

That the defense stood tall in the fourth quarter was no accident. The Wolverines kept two defining moments from the previous two seasons clearly in mind as they went through the '97 season. The first was the team's collapse a year earlier at Northwestern, when the Wolverines squandered a 16–0 lead in the fourth quarter of a 17–16 loss. The second was the defense's fourth-quarter failure at Michigan State in 1995, when the Spartans twice mounted long scoring drives to pull out a 28–25 win.

There were no repeat performances in 1997. In the first eight games, the Wolverines did not allow a point in the fourth quarter. The streak ended when Penn State scored a meaningless touchdown in the final minutes of a 34–8 Michigan triumph that vaulted the Wolverines into the top spot in the national polls.

The defense put its stamp on the season in the finale against Ohio State, when it turned away the Buckeyes on series after series to preserve a 20–14 win that clinched the outright Big Ten title and the trip to the Rose Bowl. "Even when we had the ball, I was saying, 'Let's just punt it and get our defense back out there,' " Carr said.

The offense had its moments, as well, especially late in the season when a young line gained experience and confidence. The Wolverines were virtually unstoppable in the win at Penn State. A week later at Wisconsin, the offense kept the ball out of the Badgers' hands during a 26–16 win that clinched a share of the Big Ten championship.

The trigger man for the offense was fifth-year senior quarterback Brian Griese, who'd been only a part-time starter the previous two seasons, and who'd been briefly suspended from the team the spring before the 1996 season after smashing a window at a campus bar. With no assurances that he'd be the starter in 1997, Griese wrestled with the decision whether to return for a fifth season or get on with a career in international finance. He returned, and having learned from his experiences and failures, he turned in the fifth-best passing season in school history and became the first Michigan quarterback to lead his team to three wins against Ohio State.

"Once I made the decision, I never looked back on it," Griese said after he'd been named the most valuable player in the Rose Bowl. "I never regretted it. This season was a once-in-a-lifetime opportunity. I might have regretted it if I had not come back, and we'd had this kind of season."

Michigan's championship season was one marked by resiliency, and no player embodied that more than Griese did in a 28–24 win against Iowa in mid-October. That come-from-behind victory, players and coaches agreed, was the

turning point of the season. It definitely was the Wolverines' closest call.

Griese endured a horrible first half as the Wolverines fell behind, 21–7, at intermission. He threw three of his five regular-season interceptions right to Iowa defenders. But he never lost confidence in himself. The important thing, he said, was to play better in the second half. The difference in Griese's halves was dramatic: He was eight of sixteen passing for 92 yards, a touchdown, and the three interceptions in the first half; he was seven of ten passing for 73 yards, two touchdowns, and no interceptions in the second half.

"Brian just doesn't get rattled," Carr said after the Iowa game. "I went up to him at the start of the third quarter and told him, 'This is why you're here. This is your time to take this team and bring us back.' "

The offense was remarkably balanced. With sixteen players catching passes, the first time that had happened since 1962, the Wolverines threw for 52 percent of their total yards. Senior running back Chris Howard led the team in receptions. Junior tight end Jerame Tuman, who became Griese's favorite and most dependable receiver, had the most receiving yards.

The running game was handled by committee. Howard had four 100-yard rushing games and was twice named Big Ten offensive player of the week. Junior Clarence Williams and freshman Anthony Thomas, who would eventually finish his career as Michigan's all-time leading rusher, also shared the load. Floyd's blocking saved Griese's head time and time again.

Michigan strong safety Marcus Ray (29) upends Ohio State wide receiver David Boston during the 1997 game at Michigan Stadium. The 20–14 win sent the Wolverines to the Rose Bowl. (Ann Arbor News)

The Turning Point

Both the perfect record and the Cinderella season were in jeopardy in mid-October. Number fifteen Iowa had a 21–7 halftime lead, and Michigan was struggling. But the Wolverines never doubted themselves, and they stormed back to pull out a 27–24 victory.

Coach Lloyd Carr had just a few words to say during intermission. Linebacker Sam Sword recalled the talk: "Coach Carr asked us if there was anyone in the room who didn't think we could come back. We all knew we could. We rallied around each other. We knew we'd be all right if we just hung together."

The game proved to be one of two decidedly different halves, and no player embodied that more than quarterback Brian Griese. He threw three interceptions in the first half—half his season total— then directed the Wolverines to three scoring drives in the second half. His 2-yard touchdown pass to tight end Jerame Tuman with 2:55 remaining provided the winning points. It was the first time Michigan had led all afternoon.

"Obviously, that first half was my worst since I've been here, but I never lost confidence in myself," Griese said. "I never lost confidence in the offense, either."

When Carr was asked after the game whether he considered replacing Griese, his response was to the point: "Are you crazy? But I was going to kill him."

The team's most exciting player and its inspiration was Woodson, who would win just about every individual award for which he was eligible. As brilliant as he was as a cornerback, he was nearly as good as a receiver and a punt returner.

Woodson began to creep into the national sports consciousness in late October, when he made a leaping, one-handed interception along the sidelines at Michigan State. Then, after telling sportswriters the week before the Ohio State game that he was, indeed, the best player in the nation, he eloquently backed up his argument with a brilliant performance against the Buckeyes. His 37-yard reception set up Michigan's first touchdown, and his 78-yard punt return accounted for the second touchdown. He ended Ohio State's first scoring threat with an interception in the end zone.

"He certainly played one of his greatest games in our biggest game, which is what you expect from a great player," Carr said of Woodson.

If Woodson was the team's catalyst, then Carr was its steadying influence. In his two previous seasons, Carr had learned—the hard way—that the head coach's first responsibility was to make certain his players were prepared to play on Saturday. Unlike his first two teams, the 1997 squad maintained its focus, intensity, and execution each week.

Penn State's Coach Joe Paterno remarked on that fact many times as he previewed the early November showdown between his number three Nittany Lions and fourth-ranked Michigan. The Wolverines were talented, he said, and that made them scary. What made them tough to beat, he added, was the fact that they were so well schooled and well disciplined that they could not be counted on to beat themselves.

After the game Paterno said: "Michigan is as good as anybody in the country and has as much right to be voted number one as any team in the country. They're an awfully good football team."

Few observers thought so at the beginning of the season. The Wolverines were thirteenth in the preseason writers' poll, but they'd dropped a spot by the time they opened the season in mid-September against number eight Colorado. Michigan jumped to the eighth spot with an impressive win against the Buffaloes, and it remained among the nation's top ten teams the rest of the way.

The magnitude of the win against Colorado was eye opening, and it put the nation on notice that Michigan's days of mediocrity were over. The defense held the Buffaloes to their lowest point total in nearly a decade. The offense averaged 6 yards a play in accumulating 426 total yards. "It was not an easy game, but we made it look easy," Carr said. Colorado coach Rick Neuheisel offered an even more succinct evaluation: "We got our tails whipped."

The Wolverines' close call against Notre Dame was sandwiched between easy wins against Baylor (38–3) and Indiana (37–0). Those games demonstrated much about Michigan's resolve. Unlike past seasons, where games against a lightly regarded opponent often meant a daylong struggle for Michigan, the Wolverines dispatched the Bears and Hoosiers with strong effort and solid execution.

Michigan also delivered a few paybacks en route to Pasadena. A 23–6 win against Northwestern was the Wolverines' first in three seasons. They won at Michigan State (23–7) for the first time since 1991. The win against Penn State ended a three-game losing streak to the Nittany Lions.

"I'll tell you what: You watch us the rest of the season," Ray said following the Penn State game. "We had a lot to prove. Nobody respected this team two months ago. Nobody gave us a chance. Everybody said we were mediocre. We knew all we had to do was stick together and believe in each other, and we could do whatever we wanted to do. We're not going to let up."

The Wolverines jumped to the number one ranking in the Associated Press media poll the day after the Penn State game. The coaches in the ESPN/USA Today Poll would make Michigan their top team following the win against Ohio State. No team rated number one going into the bowls and finishing with a victory had ever lost that ranking. That was about to change.

Michigan forged its 21–16 triumph against eighth-ranked Washington State in the Rose Bowl the same way it had won so often during the regular season: with tough defense and opportunistic offense.

The defense gave up 331 passing yards to Washington State star quarterback Ryan Leaf—a Heisman finalist—but the Cougars managed nowhere near their 42 points-per-game scoring average. Woodson thwarted Washington State's second scoring threat with an interception in the end zone. He also delivered a 15-yard punt return that set up Michigan's first scoring drive, and he had two critical catches for first downs during the Wolverines' final time-consuming drive.

Griese overshadowed both Woodson and Leaf, earning game MVP honors in the process. He completed eighteen of thirty passes for 251 yards and three touchdowns. His arm strength had been questioned before the game, but he answered with touchdown bombs of 53 and 58 yards to junior wide receiver Tai Streets. Griese's game-winning touchdown pass, a 23-yarder to Tuman, came off a bootleg—almost a carbon copy of the touchdown pass Griese threw to Tuman to win the Iowa game.

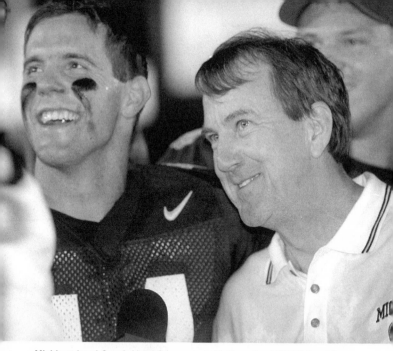

Michigan head Coach Lloyd Carr poses with Rose Bowl MVP Brian Griese (left) and captain John Jansen after the Wolverines' 21–16 win against Washington State in the Rose Bowl. (Ann Arbor News)

The offense was at its best during its final drive. Taking over at its 19 yard line with 7:25 remaining, Michigan moved 51 yards in fifteen plays to knock 6:56 off the clock. The Wolverines, who had been zero for five on third-down conversions in the first half, converted on four third downs during the final drive.

The Cougars got the ball back on their own 7 with twenty-nine seconds remaining, and Leaf nearly made the most of that time. He drove his offense 77 yards to the Michigan 16 with two seconds remaining, but time expired as he spiked a first-down pass, setting off a wild Michigan celebration and leaving the Cougars confused and frustrated.

The Wolverines felt somewhat the same way two days later when the final polls were announced. Michigan was still number one in the Associated Press poll. It would also be crowned national champion by the National Football Foundation and the Football Writers Association of America. Inexplicably, enough coaches changed their minds about the Wolverines to give Nebraska the top spot in their poll.

Still, the Wolverines had proven their point. They'd delivered a season to remember and, in the process, erased all doubt about the quality of the storied Michigan program.

"You have opportunities in your life to be something special, and this was one of them," Griese said after the Rose Bowl. "Those who stand out are the ones who make the most of those opportunities. Each and every guy on this team realized that. We capitalized on our chance to make history."

The 1997 Season

Date	Opponent	Result
September 13	vs. Colorado	W, 27–3
September 20	vs. Baylor	W, 38–3
September 27	vs. Notre Dame	W, 21–14
October 4	at Indiana	W, 37–0
October 11	vs. Northwestern	W, 23–6
October 18	vs. Iowa	W, 27–24
October 25	at Michigan St.	W, 23–7
November 1	vs. Minnesota	W, 24–3
November 8	at Penn State	W, 34–8
November 15	at Wisconsin	W, 26–16
November 22	vs. Ohio State	W, 20–14
January 1	vs. Wash. State	W, 21–16

About the Author

Jim Cnockaert has been the Michigan Wolverines beat writer for the *Ann Arbor News* since 1992. He is also coauthor of *The Road to No. 1: The Michigan Wolverines' Unforgettable Championship Season*. A native of Grosse Pointe Woods, Michigan, Cnockaert is married to fellow journalist Christine Uthoff and has three daughters: Anne, Susan, and Emily.